EUNICE

ABUNDANT GRACE

A Missionary's Testimony

by
HANS BOUWMAN

OCTOBER 1995
Published by
GOSPEL TRACT PUBLICATIONS
85 Portman Street, Glasgow G41 1EJ

ISBN 0 948417 71 4
Copyright © G.T.P., 1995

OCTOBER 1995
Printed by
GOSPEL TRACT PUBLICATIONS
85 Portman Street, Glasgow G41 1EJ

DEDICATED

to my dear wife Gerda

my best and true helpmeet in the Lord's work

to my dear children

Linda, Carla, Monica and Robert

IN MEMORIAM

of my dear daughter Marion

who went to be with the Lord

on November 15, 1988

Index of Photographs

Holland	6	Baptism in a mountain river	79
Landscape in Holland	15	A fishmonger at Utsunomiya	81
Mr and Mrs Peter Wilson	15	After the breaking of bread	81
Miss Emmy Treasure	15	Yajima San	85
"Auswitz"	21	A baptism in a river	87
German P.O.W.'s	25	Speaking at a baptism	87
Dropping food parcels	27	House meeting at Kanuma	89
Liberation by Allied Forces	29	Sunday school class	89
Surrender of German soldiers	31	Sunday school treat	91
Liberation—never to forget!	35	Gospel Hall in Korea	93
Victory Parade	35	Conference at Tokyo	93
Hilversum Conference	38	Reception to honour Gerda	95
Bible students and teachers	41	With Mr and Mrs Lou Swaan	106
Gerda Hengeveld	45	Tent meetings	107
Corrie ten Boom	45	A missionary report meeting	109
Cargo-ship to Japan	51	Assemblies in Japan	113
Japanese fishermen	55	Assemblies in Japan	115
Our first Sunday at Kobe	55	Assemblies in Japan	117
Temple worship	63	Bible-study	119
Our children in 1977	69	Bible-study	120
Assemblies in Japan 1959	73	Sitting on the *tatami*	121
"Japan-Missionary"	75	Our daughter Marion Dora	125
Living at Karuizawa	77	Serving the best of Masters	133

Holland

Contents

Acknowledgement 9
Introduction by J.B. Currie 11

Chapter 1 EARLY YEARS OF LIFE 13
—Missionaries in Holland 14

Chapter 2 THE DARK YEARS OF WAR 19
—Persecution of the Jews 19
—Persecution of the Dutch 22
—Underground Activity 23
—'D-Day' and Arnhem's Tragedy 24
—Hunger Winter 26
—Into Hiding 34
—Liberation Day 34

Chapter 3 THE CHANGE IN MY LIFE 37

Chapter 4 PREPARATION FOR FULL-TIME SERVICE 40
—Corrie Ten Boom 43
—An Important Matter 46

Chapter 5 BY FREIGHTER TO JAPAN 49
—Nature's Wonder and Power................. 49
—Entry into Japan 52
—My Fiancee's Arrival and our Wedding 54

Chapter 6 HOW WE GOT TO KNOW JAPAN 57
—The Country and its People 57
—Contact with the West 59
—Customs................................... 59
—Religion 61
—Service 64
—Competition 65
—Politeness................................. 66
—Discussions 67
—Discrimination 68

Chapter 7 PARTICIPATION IN MISSIONARY WORK 71
—Reaching out to the Japanese 71
—Pioneer Work 74
—First Fruits................................. 80
—Other Cities Reached 83
—Leprosy Camp 86
—The Next Move 88
—Gospel Work in Korea...................... 88
—The Dutch Community in Japan 90
—Sayonara—Farewell 92

Chapter 8 ORGANIZATIONAL DIFFICULTIES 96
—Unwritten Rules 97
—God's School............................... 99
—God's Miracles 100

Chapter 9 CANADA—A NEW HOME COUNTRY 102
—Becoming Canadians 104

Chapter 10 HOLLAND—A NEW SPHERE OF LABOUR ... 105
—The Great Need 108
—Opportunities Granted 108
—Publication Work 111

Chapter 11 REVISITING JAPAN 112

Chapter 12 MEMORIES OF A PRECIOUS DAUGHTER ... 124
—Marion's Testimony........................ 126
—Alan's Words of Appreciation 129

Chapter 13 CONCLUSION 130
—Scriptural Principles 130
—The Lord's Call 130
—Responsibility of the Assembly 131
—Commendation 132
—A Work of God 132
—Heaven's Reward 134

Acknowledgement

"... that the ABUNDANT GRACE might through the thanks-giving of many redound to the glory of God" (2 Cor.4:15b).

Realizing that each servant of the Lord could write a book about all the remarkable experiences in the Lord's work, these pages are written with a great deal of reservation and hesitation. In the final analysis, each life lived for the Lord is unique, and even the smallest service done for Him is special, because it will be valued and marked for eternity. "For God is not unrighteous to forget your work and labour of love, which ye have shown toward His Name" (Heb.6:10).

As I am privileged to be in various assemblies for missionary reports, ministry and Gospel meetings, I have frequently used illustrations from my life's experience. It has been repeatedly suggested that I collect these experiences in writing with a view to publication, in the Lord's will.

My daughter Marion offered her help in doing the editing. However, after finishing the first two chapters, she became seriously ill with cancer, and in 1988 she entered into the presence of the Lord. Some years later I felt led to go ahead with the proposed project and I am very thankful to have found others willing to assist. I am much indebted to them for their willingness to sacrifice of their time and effort.

'A Missionary's Testimony' is presented with the prayer that it may be a blessing and an encouragement for the reader, especially for those who seek to serve the Lord. Looking back over 40 years of missionary service, the only thing which counts is a conviction regarding the call of the Lord. Being assured of the call, we have sought to be faithful in fulfilling our task. In spite of our own weakness, our faithful God has blessed and used us, all because of His abundant grace. "Faithful is He that calleth you, who also will do it" (1 Thess.5:24).

REMARK
The word 'assembly' is repeatedly used in this book. Though

9

the word 'church' is commonly used, we prefer the word
'assembly', since it is a better expression of the Greek word
ecclesia, a called-out-people. In its local aspect, the assembly is a
company of Christians gathered together in the Name of the
Lord Jesus Christ, where the Lordship of Christ is recognized.

Introduction

An autobiography is meant to tell a very personal story. The little book by our brother Hans Bouwman does this very well indeed. It is both interesting and readable but, more importantly, it tells the story of God's gracious dealings in the growth of a soul.

I have, in different ways, been linked with Hans and his wife Gerda since ever they arrived in Japan at the start of their missionary career. Many of the ups and downs, the joys and the sorrows they have experienced were known to me as they actually happened. On occasions I was asked for advice and help which, I sincerely pray, was of some encouragement to them in the twists and turns they had to follow in their years of service for God.

It seemed rather strange to me that God would bring a young man all the way from his native Holland and, after years of 'training in God's school', just at the time when it seemed he and his wife were at the pinnacle of their usefulness for God in the very needy land of Japan, that He would send them, by way of Canada, back to work in Holland. I told Hans this at the time he first broached the subject to tell me of his exercise. It soon became evident that I was very wrong in my estimate of the situation. God has given Hans and Gerda a work to do in Holland, no doubt, for which the years in Japan have amply prepared them. In spite of the great need here in Japan I would say that they are meeting an even greater need in Holland. Two necessary lessons are emphasised in this. It never does to try and get 'guidance' for someone else and, conventional wisdom is not necessarily in keeping with God's mind for His servants.

Not given to reading biographies very much I approached 'ABUNDANT GRACE' with the thought, 'I can't spare time for this'. I am glad I did! Now I can heartily recommend the book to all the Lord's people, especially those who are gathered to the Name of the Lord Jesus in assembly capacity. It not only tells a very personal story but it also gives much information about the work of the Lord here in Japan.

May God richly bless the little book and use it to glorify the Name of our Lord Jesus Christ.

Tokyo, April 10th 1995

CHAPTER ONE

Early Years of Life

It was a very cold winter and the freezing weather had come to Holland much earlier than usual. Canals and lakes were frozen solid, and the 'Hollanders' made good use of their ice-skates. Children criss-crossed the ice to go to school, and the adults also used this cheap transportation to get to work. Cities like Amsterdam with its many canals portrayed cozy Dutch winter scenery. In the late afternoons, both young and old glided across the ice for pleasure. Here and there along the canals, little canvas stalls were set up to sell the famous Dutch hot chocolate, which was a nice treat in the cold and windy weather.

It was in this gripping winter of 1928 that I was born as the youngest of four children. I was born of parents who knew the Lord Jesus Christ as their Lord and Saviour. Their conversion had occurred only three years before. My parents had always been religious people who went faithfully to church, and my father read the Bible daily at the table, and prayers were said. My mother was from a large Roman Catholic family of nine children. When she married a Protestant, her family broke off all ties, and she was completely ignored, if not forgotten. Having deserted the 'one true church', she was treated as an apostate, and as a small boy I often wondered why her relatives never came to our birthdays and holiday get-togethers. It was only years later that the enmity gradually thawed and contact was re-established. It was very nice to get to know the many relatives, especially grandmother. She was living right in the centre of Utrecht, a big city in the middle of the country. The little alley opposite the railway station with its small houses is still there today, and I remember that little cottage so well where I thoroughly enjoyed the baking and cooking of my grandmother.

Missionaries in Holland

One day in 1925 while my mother was doing her shopping, she was kindly invited to attend Gospel meetings which were being conducted in a public hall. With two young children at home, my parents could not attend the meetings together, so they decided to take turns. A gentleman from Scotland was the preacher, and my parents were quickly impressed by the simple presentation of Scriptures concerning salvation. They had never heard the Gospel preached like this in their church, and now for the first time they became deeply concerned about their souls' salvation. It was during these meetings that they realized that religion could not save them, but that only the Lord Jesus Christ could. Under much opposition they left the denominational church and joined themselves to the company of believers, gathered unto the Name of our Lord Jesus Christ.

The preacher, Mr. Peter Wilson, was born in 1876 in a little place called Chirnside in Scotland. He felt called by the Lord to serve as a missionary, and at age 25 he sailed to Sarawak on the north-west coast of Borneo, at that time a British colony. Mr. Wilson's desire was to eventually go into the Dutch part of Borneo (the former Dutch East-Indies). With this in mind he had already learned the Dutch language while in Scotland. However, the Lord did not allow him to realize his ambitious plans. Ill-health compelled Mr. Wilson to leave Borneo prematurely, and as he was not able to undertake the long sea journey back to Scotland, he sailed instead to a new country, New Zealand. There he started a new chapter in his personal life. After his health had improved, he married Miss Ethel Rose Brice. Both had a deep interest for the Lord's work in the Netherlands, and it was not long before this compelled them to sail from New Zealand to Europe.

Just before the outbreak of the First World War in 1914 they moved to Holland. Because of its neutrality in the on-going war, many refugees from different parts of Europe had fled to Holland. As a result, Mr. Wilson received permission from the authorities to be the 'chaplain' in refugee camps. Thousands of refugees in great despair heard the Gospel preached to them, and many accepted the call and got saved. Only eternity can show the result of this great work.

After the war the Wilsons moved back to Scotland to wait for

Landscape in Holland

Mr. and Mrs. Peter Wilson   *Miss Emmy Treasure from New Zealand*
from Scotland

further indications of the Lord's guidance. In 1920 they returned to Holland, but this time to settle as the Lord's servants among the Dutch people, where their efforts were really blessed. Mr. Wilson saw many people saved, especially in the north-eastern part, which was the poorest area of the country. The local people there made a living as turf-cutters, cutting pieces of peat to be used in the old-fashioned kitchen stoves. To reach these rough men, most of whom were communists, Mr. Wilson even went into the cafés (like a bar today) to talk to them. Despite the rough and godless atmosphere, the Lord was able to soften many a stony heart. A time of revival ensued, and many of these people accepted the Lord Jesus Christ as their Saviour. The rough day-labourers were simple and direct in their speech but powerful in their testimonies, for in poor circumstances they had a deep experience of the love and care of the Lord.

In the western part of the Netherlands also, Mr. Wilson held Gospel meetings which resulted in the conversion of many people. These Christians continued in the 'ways of the Lord', and after being baptized they were added to the fellowship of local assemblies, which spontaneously came into existence in the various places where the gospel had been preached.

Mr. Wilson went to be with the Lord in 1951. Even today there are still a few older Christians who were saved through the powerful preaching of this servant of the Lord, who showed such a great love and concern for the Dutch people.

Another missionary, Miss Emmy Treasure from New Zealand, lived for some years in Holland to help the Wilsons in their efforts to proclaim the Gospel, and she was very active in reaching the children. I remember being in her Sunday school class as a young child. These were the missionaries at a time when Holland was in need of the simple Gospel.

After my parents heard the gospel preached by Peter Wilson and became Christians, they were ostracized by the people in their former church. The pastor continued his visits for a time in an attempt to keep his sheep in the fold. But having entered into an assembly of the Lord's people, they enjoyed the fellowship with the believers who really cared for them. Having a conviction about the place where the Lord dwells among His people, there was for them no return to a traditional church where the Gospel had been lost.

I had a happy childhood. As a boy I loved to play outside in the fields or in the woods and to sail my toy boat on the lake. Going to my father's workshop was fun too, as he would often let me play with scraps of wood. My father was a hard worker who spent many long hours in his carpentry workshop, and he was able, though with difficulty, to maintain his business through the years of depression. He took pride in his work, thus giving it the quality that generated customer demand even in those hard times.

My carefree, happy childhood came to an end on May 10, 1940. My father woke early in the morning to the sound of airplanes and went into the livingroom to turn on the radio. What he suspected had become reality: war had broken out for Holland! It was not long until we were all listening to the continuous special news bulletins. The German army had crossed the Dutch border at 3 a.m. in the morning. The Dutch soldiers were facing a well disciplined and very powerful force. There was severe fighting to hold the first line of defence in the east of the country. When the Germans pushed through, the Dutch army retreated behind the 'Holland Water Defence Line', made up of lakes, rivers and inundated land. To retreat to this area, the Dutch army had to pass through our street during the night of the 13th of May. It impressed us so much to see the exhaustion of the soldiers, who had fought for four days and were still fighting against an overwhelming power. Everyone knew that it was of no use to continue any longer, especially after German planes bombed the city of Rotterdam. This was in the afternoon at 2 p.m. on the 14th of May.

During the occupation, as a sign of a silent demonstration, in many homes the curtains were closed for an hour on the 14th of May from 2 p.m. till 3 p.m. The bombing of Rotterdam was done on an open city, without any military target. The ultimatum singled out other cities to be bombed unless there was an unconditional surrender, and that happened in the early hours of a beautiful evening on the 14th of May 1940. This day is one of the most tragic days in the history of the Netherlands. Already during the time of mobilization, loudspeakers were located at strategic spots in the city for the mayor to address the people. During the days of fighting, the mayor would speak to the people every evening at 7 p.m. This is how we heard the news that the Dutch Commander-in-Chief had capitulated to the Germans. I remember that there was complete silence in the streets and in the houses. Then there was crying, especially over the unknown future. Little did we realize that the five days of fighting would be followed by five terrible years of occupation!

CHAPTER TWO

The Dark Years of the War

As a young boy I was somehow caught up in the excitement of the war. During the mobilization of the Dutch army in 1939, I often had played 'soldiers' with my friends. Now, however, we saw the real thing. I remember the German army entering our city and occupying the radio stations and other important buildings and factories. As time went on I increasingly realized the horror of war.

For our family the first few years of occupation were not so bad. Although food was rationed, there was still sufficient to eat. However, the persecution of the Jews was a great shock for the Dutch people. Bram, one of my neighbourhood friends, was a Jew and it was through him and his family that I shared in some of the helpless fear they constantly faced.

Persecution of the Jews

The tragic 'Kristallnacht' of November 9, 1938 was the beginning of the persecution of the Jews under the Nazi regime in Germany. During that night the shops, factories and houses of Jews all over Germany were attacked, damaged or set on fire. During that night about 200 Jews were killed, and from then on many Jews sought refuge in other countries. Assuming that Holland would stay neutral, as it did in the First World War, many had fled there and found a welcome. Dutch history is full of instances where Holland became a haven for people who were persecuted because of their race or faith. At the outbreak of the Second World War there was a large Jewish population living in Holland, especially in the big cities like Amsterdam, Rotterdam, and The Hague.

When persecution started in Holland, the Jews were marked out by a large orange 'Star of David', which had to be visibly worn on their clothes at all times. Public places like theatres, cinemas, parks, recreational centres, hotels and restaurants were prohibited to Jews. Gradually they became the target of Hitler's plan to exterminate the Jewish race. They were arrested and the process of deportation to the concentration camps began.

One morning a German truck drove into our street and stopped in front of Bram's house. It was heartbreaking to see this family of five, including a baby, being herded like cattle into an army truck. Bram looked towards our house as he climbed into the truck, and I could see the look of fear and helplessness on his face. Again a family deported to an 'unknown' destination. As we peeped through the curtain to watch, my father said, "For these people there will be no return". But he added words of comfort: "Hitler may do what he wants, and he may win many battles, but in the end he will lose the war, because he is persecuting the Jews, who belong to God's chosen nation".

In 1986 I was in Poland together with a brother from England offering the Christians material and spiritual help. While we were there a Polish brother took us out to Auschwitz. As we stood in front of the former concentration camp, this brother asked me whether I wanted to go inside, and I remember how I hesitated before giving an answer. Though I had not experienced the Nazi barbarities of a concentration camp myself, it certainly would bring back memories of the awful scenes of deportation, including those of my good friend Bram. We entered the iron gate above which the slogan was written 'ARBEIT MACHT FREI', which means 'LABOUR SETS FREE'. As we went inside and strolled through the barracks, I thought about the desperate condition in which these people suffered during their last days on earth. We also stood still at the 'Death Wall', the place where every day at the early morning roll-call a number of Jews were shot to death, while all the others had to watch the execution. We entered the gas chambers and there I stood in the very place where Jews by the thousands had met an untimely death. Above the entrance door was a sign reading, 'Shower Room'. It was there that they went through the door, naked, with a little piece of soap and a towel in their hands, assuming that they were about to take a shower. But instead of water, poison gas came out of the pipes to kill them! It is said that a gas chamber could kill 1,500 to 2,000 people at a time. After fifteen

Entrance of Death-Camp "Auswitz".
Above the entrance-gate is written:
"Arbeit macht frei" ("Labour liberates")

The "Death-Wall" of concentration camp "Auswitz",
where each morning people were executed for "misbehaviour".
Today it stands as a memorial

or twenty minutes all were dead and their bodies were burnt in crematoria or even at stakes. I could not look at all the evidences of torture and killing with dry eyes, realizing that no less than four million victims found their death. Behind huge glass windows were heaps of shoes, old fashioned glasses, dentures, shaving brushes and, what I felt to be most shocking, all the hair of the shaved victims. It was a terrible sight! This concentration camp, like so many others, was a place of sorrow and pain, of horror and inhumanity on an incredible scale.

In Holland not one Jew was seen in the streets anymore. Nearly all were deported, fortunately some were able to go into hiding with the help of the Dutch people. At the end of the war only 5,000 Dutch Jews survived of the many who were sent to the concentration camps, where the inhuman practices of the Nazis were carried out to try and exterminate the Jewish race.

Persecution of the Dutch

After the Germans had settled the Jewish problem, life became difficult for the Dutch people as well. It was not allowed for more than three people to meet publicly. Because of 'total war', many German soldiers were on the frontlines, and men of the occupied countries were needed to fill their places in the factories. I still remember the day when this decree was promulgated by the Chief Commander of occupied Holland— one of many! Each decree was announced on bulletin boards which were erected in different places in the city. This particular decree caused a drastic change in my life. All males aged 16 to 60 were deported to Germany and forced to work for the war industry. The only alternative was to go into hiding. Often a sudden 'razzia' would take place, a search for men who were in hiding. A whole neighbourhood would be sealed off, so that there was no chance of escape. Each house was thoroughly searched out, not only for men but also for valuables. Anything made of gold, silver, pewter or metal was confiscated and used for the war industry. During the battle of Stalingrad in the winter of 1942, as the German front lines were suffering the brutal cold of a Russian winter, the Dutch people were robbed of sweaters, pullovers, blankets or anything else that could be used by the soldiers. The Germans entered the cold bedrooms of the Dutch houses and counted the blankets. Two blankets for a bed were allowed, but any surplus was confiscated. We lost three nice woollen blankets.

Underground Activity

To prevent people from listening to the radio broadcasts of the 'enemy', all radio sets were confiscated. Just before the outbreak of the war my father had bought a new radio set. The old one was turned in, and as long as we had proof of a confiscation document in the house to show at the time of a 'razzia', we were all right. The new radio set was hidden in a secret place, but each night we took it out and listened to the Dutch broadcast of the 'Voice of America' and BBC London. It was quite a nervous and exciting time. Doors were locked, curtains pulled and the volume was set as low as possible, as we stood attentively listening to the news. We had to be very careful, because not all people could be trusted. The common saying was: 'The walls have ears'.

Things became more difficult when gas and electricity were cut off. This was also the end of listening to the news. My friend Jan, who later in life became a radio technician, had made himself a nice crystal set. It received the newscast from London and New York very clearly. Through headphones we collected the news, typed it out on an old typewriter and distributed it in a one-page bulletin to people whom we could trust. In a small way, it was an underground activity, and not without danger.

One afternoon at 4.45 p.m., as we were listening upstairs in Jan's bedroom to 'The Voice of America', we were unaware of the great danger we were in. The backdoor was not locked and three German soldiers had stepped into the house. Jan's mother was intently occupied in solving a crossword puzzle, when suddenly the soldiers burst in upon her. "Where are the men", they shouted. Even though very frightened, she did something exceptionally courageous. She ran to the stove, grabbed the poker, lifted it up and shouted, "What men? You have already taken away my husband from me and that's enough!" Some time before, Jan's father had been deported to Germany and was working in a factory at Osnabrueck. "Now, get out of my house and leave me alone!", she yelled as loudly as she could, hoping that we would hear her voice and be prepared. However, we were so much involved in our 'job' that we did not hear anything of the tumult downstairs.

The soldiers faced what they thought to be a hysterical woman and, unsure of what they should do, they stood for a few moments in complete silence, overwhelmed by such a daring scene. Then the officer in charge ordered the soldiers to leave her alone. When the soldiers were gone, Jan's mother stood trembling, as the full realization hit her of what could have happened. Coming in through the backdoor it would have been easy for the German soldiers to use the stairs to the bedroom first, but instead, they passed the stairs and had entered into the living room. What a protection of the Lord in a time of great danger! If they had found us with all the evidence of the written news from the enemy's side, we probably would not be alive today. This was one of several instances where I was clearly spared.

'D-Day' and Arnhem's Tragedy

The year of 1944 was an eventful one. On the 6th of June the Allied forces landed at Normandy in France to open up the 'Western front'. There had been a lot of speculation as to where the Allied Forces would invade the European continent. The whole coastline along western Europe was built into a powerful defence bulwark, called the 'Atlantic Wall'. Where would the invasion take place? In Norway, Denmark, Holland, Belgium or France? When 'D-Day' arrived we were so excited, knowing that the day of our liberation drew nearer than ever. During the first months, fighting was severe and many soldiers lost their lives. Then Paris was liberated and not long after that, Brussels, the capital of Belgium. Now the Allied Forces were not far from the border of Holland. On September 17, 1944, a contingent of the First Airborne division was dropped from the air near the Dutch city of Arnhem. I remember this Sunday afternoon so well. It was a bright day with a lot of sunshine. As many planes flew over our city, we were wondering what was going on. Particularly during the night we were used to hearing for hours the sound of sometimes hundreds of planes on missions to bomb cities in Germany. But now it was daytime and the planes flew much lower. It was not long before we received the news that there was an Airborne division parachuting in to engage in

American troops crossed the border to liberate the southern part of Holland

The first German P.O.W.'s in Holland

'Operation Market Garden'. The purpose of this strategy was to occupy the main bridge crossing the Rhine at Arnhem to give unhindered passage to the Allied forces from the south of Holland. More than 10,000 soldiers parachuted into territory occupied by the enemy. For the Dutch people it was such a thrill to know that our liberators were not far away, in fact only a 30 mile (45 km.) distance from our city.

It happened that at a location just north of Arnhem a strong Panzer division of the German army was present, and soon the slaughter started on the men trying to hold on to the Rhine bridge and the surrounding area. The fighting in the city of Arnhem was so severe that it became a battle over each house. Though the thrust of the Allied forces had been fast over the past weeks, here the situation changed completely. With the resistance of a reorganized and still very strong German army, the armies of the Allied forces in the south of Holland were not able to advance further north. It was a tragedy for the Airborne division to retreat after fighting so hard for a week to maintain control over the bridge. Withdrawn to a small piece of land, west of Arnhem, but still north of the Rhine, the soldiers could do nothing else but cross the river. During the night of September 25 the withdrawal started. Since the Germans were in a better position to control the Rhine, constant gunfire was directed at the men who tried to cross the river. Many were fatally shot within sight of safety and only 3,000 soldiers survived. Near Arnhem is the cemetery of the brave soldiers of the Airborne Division, who gave their lives for a military strategy which became a complete debacle. 'Operation Market Garden' is one of the greatest failures of World War II. With the title, "A Bridge too Far", this tragedy has been filmed and also published. Holland could not be liberated yet, and from then on the Allied forces tried to thrust in an eastward direction into Germany. This was also not without bloodshed, as severe fighting occurred in the Ardennes in Belgium, where today rows of white grave stones in cemetries are the silent witnesses of a cruel war.

Hunger Winter

Since the debacle of Arnhem real hardship occurred in the still occupied part of Holland. There was hardly anything available in the stores. It was the time to wear 'klompen', because leather

Dropping of food parcels for people suffering from malnutrition

Collecting the food parcels

shoes were no longer available. Wooden clogs are much used in the rural areas, but not in cities. But towards the end of the war this was the only footwear which could be bought. With a little straw inside and thick woollen socks the feet stayed nicely warm in 'klompen'. Soon the shortage of food became serious. Even with ration tickets, in use since the beginning of the war, food could not be obtained anymore. Stores had run completely out of food, and people in the big cities were struggling to keep alive. The only possibility of obtaining some food was to go out and get it from the farmers. These trips were called 'hunger trips'. Thousands of people went on foot or, if they were lucky, on old bicycles to the farming areas in the north and east of the country, covering a one-way distance of easily 100 to 160 miles (150-250 km). These trips were made under the most bizarre and dangerous circumstances. We too rode far distances to get some food, but were still fortunate to use our bicycles with massive tyres made from a strip of rubber of an old car tyre. Since money had hardly any value the farmers traded their potatoes and grain for things they wanted. My mother had still quite a lot of tea, and it was an attractive item for trading. Also, all our new bathtowels, dishcloths, sheets and ornaments were traded in. On the many 'hunger trips' I saw a lot of misery and suffering. During the five to seven day trip the nights were mostly spent in a haystack or, if we were lucky to get the farmer's permission, we were able to sleep in the barn, above the cows. On one occasion on our way back from a hunger trip, while riding through wet and foggy weather, I was completely exhausted and very thirsty. Sparkling drops of misty rain had collected on the woollen mittens which my mother had knitted, and as I licked the mittens I was so thankful for this thirst-quenching refreshment which was like dew from heaven!

The greatest danger we faced were the bombardments and shootings by the allied bombers and fighter planes on truck convoys or buildings occupied by the Germans. Unfortunately the allied bombers occasionally missed their targets, and the surrounding houses were hit. As the planes swooped down we often had to dive into a man-hole alongside the road, or flatten ourselves against the wall of a farmer's house. The noise, destruction, and death terrified me. One day a formation of 8 fighter planes attacked our city. The target was a villa where the

While waiting for the Allied Forces, the Germans were still in control

The Canadian Army entered Hilversum as our liberators

German Commander had his Headquarters. We lived some distance away and were watching the planes from the roof of our house. It was quite a sight, but how sad we were when we heard that the target had been missed and that houses of Dutch people had been bombed resulting in death and destruction. A mother ran upstairs to get her three-month-old baby out of the crib, but it was there that both were hit by ammunition fired from the planes. I was always thankful for the days when there were no attacks from the air.

On another occasion because of curfew, we had to hurry home from our hunger trip. Curfew was from 8 p.m. till 6 a.m., and since the streets were not lit, we had great difficulty staying in the bicycle lane. It was a dark night. My father and I rode as fast as we could to be home before curfew time. Suddenly I discovered that my father had disappeared. I stopped and tried to locate him, but because of the darkness I could see hardly anything. "Dad, where are you?" I called out and strained my ears to hear his voice. I heard him faintly call my name and as I looked back, I found him tangled up in his bicycle at the bottom of a deep bombshelter hole along the roadside. I helped him climb out of the hole. Fortunately his injuries were not too bad. We dragged his bicycle out and managed to straighten it out. Then we quickly continued our journey and it was exactly at the stroke of eight when we safely entered our house. We were exhausted, weak, sore, and what seemed worst of all, hungry, but we were so thankful to have some food at hand to fill our hungry stomachs!

The time came when the Germans decided to close the bridges over the Yssel river, so that the farming areas could not be reached anymore. I remember our last 'hunger trip', this time together with my sister, Jean. Approaching a small village we saw a group of people standing by the roadside. We stopped to see what the commotion was, and saw to our great surprise a big pile of slaughtered calves. It was meat destined for the German army, but an accident instigated by the underground movement had occurred. The meat was piled up along the roadside, but there were no soldiers to watch over this treasure. My sister suggested that we should take a whole calf, instead of cutting off small pieces as others were doing. I held a big sack open as my sister slid the calf into it. Whether it was a good or bad example, I

Surrender of German soldiers near my home town

German soldiers are laying down their weapons

did not know, but other people started to do the same. In a short
time the whole pile of meat was gone and there was not one calf
left for the Germans. It was pretty awkward riding my bicycle
with a calf on the back-carrier, but somehow I managed. At a
farmer's house we were able to trade some goods for potatoes
and we arranged these around the calf, so that the meat would
be hidden in the event of us being searched. Again we arrived
home safely and were able to enjoy this delicious meat with our
potatoes, a rich meal which we hadn't tasted for a long time!

From this time on there was no possibility supplementing our
food provision. What we had accumulated had to last till the end
of the war. Not knowing when the end would come there was
no guarantee that the food provision would last. With each
passing day's small ration on the table, my father always gave
thanks for a 'rich provision', which consisted of cooked sugar
beets and a few potatoes. I remember that we even vied for the
crumbs on the table, and with the wartime custom of licking our
plates clean, there was literally nothing left. During the 'hunger
winter' many people died of malnutrition, especially among the
young and the elderly. Hunger compelled people to eat their
own pets as they did not have food for the animals and were
hungry themselves. Then, when life was so bleak, the Swedish
Red Cross arranged to provide food parcels. The Germans had
agreed to this offer, and Swedish planes were allowed to drop
parcels in certain designated areas. Although the amount of
food was scarce in proportion to the heavily populated area in
the west of Holland, every little bit helped. It was even more of a
boost to the morale of the Dutch people who looked forward
with great anticipation to the end of the occupation. For the first
time in years we were able to taste white bread again. I still
remember how white it looked!

Since gas or electricity was cut off, the cooking was done on a
woodstove. The firewood was obtained by cutting trees in the
woods. Gradually, even the trees along the roadsides disappeared.
In the big cities people were so desperate that they chopped up
their cupboards, parts of stairs and even ceilings to get wood for
their stoves. At night the only light in the whole house was from
a little wick in a cup of oil. We were one of the fortunate families
in that we still had some oil on hand and needless to say, it was
very sparingly used. In the dim light it was not possible to read

or work, so instead we often sat around the table and played games to pass the time. On one occasion we were talking about the people facing starvation, and my brother Ad remarked, "I can imagine that some people would not mind being killed by a bomb, because that would be the end of their misery." No sooner had he spoken these words when a plane flew very low over our house. We were all frightened and listened in rigid suspense. Then the tremendous sound of a terrific explosion reverberated through the night. We hid under the table till the plane was gone. Some windows in our house were broken, but because of curfew we were not able to venture outside to see the damage. The next morning we saw that some houses had been hit, and a lot of glass and bricks were scattered around; two elderly people had been killed.

There was also the tragedy of planes shot down by the Germans. I remember a plane that had been shot down during the night. Our curiosity led us to the crash site near by, and we were shocked to discover a boot with a human leg still in it. From the German side the rockets known as the V1 and V2 crossed over Holland and the North Sea on their way to targets in England. There was a launch-pad built in the east of Holland and many times we saw the rockets fly through the sky. It happened sometimes that a rocket would fail and come down like a fireball, as it did one time in our city. The cruelty of war was an increasing reality.

The suffering in Holland was not only felt in material things, but far more in respect to life itself. There was a very active underground resistance going on, and to suppress the underground's activities, the Germans knew how to use effective reprisals. For one German killed, ten innocent Dutch people were shot to death as an act of retaliation. This could happen unexpectedly while people in the street were forced to watch the execution. Many towns and cities have a monument as a grim reminder of these tragic executions. One night, not far from where we lived, there was an attack by the underground movement during which a German general was injured. The retaliation was nothing short of dreadful. All the men of the town where the attack had occurred were dragged out of their houses and shot to death.

Into Hiding

When I turned 16 my life changed drastically. I was forced to make a choice of reporting to the Germans for work duty or going into hiding. My oldest brother, Jo, had gone into hiding a few years earlier, but unfortunately he had been caught in 1943 and was deported to a labour camp in Germany. We did not hear about him until some weeks after the war had ended, when we were at last informed by the Red Cross that he was alive and recuperating in France from the maltreatment suffered under the Germans. Three months after the capitulation of Germany in the beginning of May 1945, he was able to return home. Because of my brother's discovery and transfer to a labour camp, I lived in constant fear whilst I was in hiding. My father, being a carpenter, had made a 'professional' hiding place underneath the house. It could be entered by a trapdoor in the floor of a small closet. The space underneath the house was only two feet high, and it was very draughty and uncomfortable. I slept on a thin mattress placed on the sand and hoped it would be a secure place. It happened quite often that during a 'razzia' German soldiers searched for men one house after the other and sometimes used their pistols to shoot through walls, floors and ceilings. These 'razzias' were very frightening, and I hardly dared to breathe under the pounding of German boots above my head.

Liberation Day

The spring of 1945 was beautiful, but being in hiding I did not get a chance to enjoy it. Rumours abounded during those days, and we often heard of both defeats and victories that were untrue. On the fifth of May, however, rumour became reality! At around 7.30 p.m. a few people ran out of their houses, grabbed each other's hands and were jumping around for joy. This was the moment we had longed for, for so long. We realized what it meant—liberation! In only a few moments the main street on which I lived was filled with people. The atmosphere outside was lively and happy as people hugged, cried, and laughed. At around nine in the evening we suddenly heard gunshots from the Germans who were still in power. They ordered everyone off the streets within five minutes, as we were still obliged to keep to curfew time. In a matter of

Liberation–never to forget!

Victory Parade of the Royal Canadian Army

moments the streets were desolate again, but how good it felt to have tasted something of our liberation, which now was just around the corner. That night I did not need to go into my hiding place anymore; I could sleep in my own bed without fear.

CHAPTER THREE

The Change in My Life

Holland was free again and the liberation celebrations continued for almost half a year. Neighbourhoods took turns organizing festivals for children and adults and I also joined the crowds and began to enjoy the new found 'freedom'. In highschool I played the guitar in a school orchestra, and later I joined a dance band which played gigs in the dance halls each weekend. Saturdays and Sundays I came home at the earliest at 2 a.m., but often much later. I would lie down exhausted after another night of enjoying the pleasures of the world. This was 'night life' with no time left to think about spiritual things, but the Lord did not distance Himself from me. I had parents who prayed that the Gospel, which I knew well, might have its effect in my life. And, indeed, gradually it dawned on me that there was no satisfaction whatsoever in the kind of life I tried to enjoy. It was a strange discovery, for in spite of the many friends surrounding me, I felt more and more alone, and all the pleasures and fun only produced an emptiness in my heart. The more I considered it, the more restless I became.

On a beautiful Sunday afternoon in September of 1948 I decided to go out for a bicycle ride. Rarely did I want to be on my own, but I did on this particular afternoon. Riding my bicycle through the beautiful forests and the fields of purple heather I arrived in the next town. Suddenly I realized that I was quite near a Gospel Hall. I looked at my watch and knew that soon the Gospel meeting would start. "What about it?", I thought by myself, "Just go and see!" The hall was filling up with people, and because I had not entered a Gospel Hall for about 5 years, I felt like a stranger among them. I found out that a baptism was to take place, and the little hall was filled to capacity. The meeting started and soon I witnessed the baptism of five young people, all about my age. The preacher spoke on the subject: 'What a Christian possesses in Christ, his Lord'. It was an

Conference convened by my home assembly at Hilversum
(I stand in the right top corner)

impressive message and I felt that it was spoken directly to me. All that was lacking in my life—joy, peace, satisfaction—could only be found in Christ. lost sinner in need of salvation. After the end of the meeting I hurried out of the hall as I had no desire to meet the Christians. I returned home, threw my bicycle into the shed, ran upstairs to my little bedroom and there surrendered myself in accepting the Lord Jesus Christ as my Saviour. I thought back to the Liberation Day, three years previously, when Holland was freed from the yoke of a terrible occupation. But I had just experienced a far greater liberation. How wonderful to be assured of the forgiveness of sins and to be set free from its bondage! The Lord Jesus had paid the ransom for my sins, and the price had been paid to set a slave free—"If the Son therefore shall make you free, ye shall be free indeed" (John 8:36).

Four months later on December 31 of 1948, I was baptized in that same Gospel Hall where I had witnessed the baptism that had led to my salvation. This time I was the only one to be baptized, but how happy I felt in taking this step of obedience!

The *Gospel* is emphasized by the word TO—'Come to Me!'

The *position* of a Christian is emphasized by the word IN—'Saints in Christ Jesus'.

Baptism is emphasized by the word WITH—identification with Christ in His death, burial and resurrection.

CHAPTER FOUR

Preparation for Full-Time Service

A few weeks after my baptism I was received into the fellowship of an assembly which had been established in 1925 as a result of Mr. Peter Wilson's Gospel preaching. A happy and joyful spirit existed among the assemblies in Holland, and I remember how I was especially blessed during the time of conferences. However, after Mr. Peter Wilson went to be with the Lord in 1950, the assemblies were left with only a few brethren capable of ministering the Word of God. As time went by it became more and more evident that there was a great lack of teaching Scriptural principles concerning the truth of gathering unto the Lord's Name. Increasingly, the assemblies lost their identity and the Christians became restless and unhappy, so that some even left. Unfortunately in some cases whole assemblies became denominational churches. It was a time when conviction became weaker, due to a lack of appeal to "earnestly contend for the faith, which was once delivered unto the saints" (Jude 3). As I was still young I did not realize the impact of these developments. I desired to be active for the Lord and participated in all the activities of the assembly. These included regular tract distribution, open-air meetings, Gospel outreach in hospitals, senior citizens homes and a nearby gypsy camp. I always felt happy when I could speak about the great love of the Saviour and what a joy it was to sing together of our blessed Redeemer!

In fellowship with the assemblies in Holland and Belgium, I felt led to organize a Gospel tour through Belgium during the summer of 1952. Being confident of the Lord's guidance we set out on our long bicycle tour with twenty young people. We carried a good supply of tracts and, after crossing the border, we went from place to place conducting open-air meetings in the market square or at street corners. Thousands of tracts were distributed, and in contacting the people we experienced

Bible students with teachers:
Mr. Erich Sauer, Mr. Ernst Schrupp, Mr. Heinz Kohler

wonderful opportunities to testify about the living Saviour. In
the evenings we enjoyed the sweet hospitality of the Christians
from the Belgian assemblies. On many occasions these
Christians joined us in the open-air work to make Christ known
to a people bound in the superstition of Roman Catholicism.

It was during this time that I felt the Lord speaking to me.
Increasingly my thoughts were occupied with what it could
mean to serve the Lord full-time. Not long after, I plucked up
courage to speak about my burden to the elders of my home
assembly. I was very happy to find a listening ear and to have
their understanding. However, since I would be the first
missionary from Dutch assemblies, the brethren did not exactly
know what to advise me. It was suggested that I should go to a
Bible school, preferably to the one run by assemblies in
Germany. "Without training you cannot go out as a missionary",
was their reasoning. Being still young, I accepted the advice of
the respected elders, but in the course of my life's experience
and with an increasing conviction about the principles of the
New Testament, I realized later that the training ground to
become a missionary is not a Bible school or a theological
seminary, but the local assembly. It is evident that training in an
institution can even spoil the simplicity of God's Plan
manifested in Holy Scripture.

According to Scripture the potential to be used in the Lord's
service lies in proper fellowship with a local assembly, since this
is the place where He dwells in the midst of His people.
Certainly an assembly is not perfect and it could manifest
various weaknesses and imperfections, but if God's Word is
recognized as the only source of authority, all the spiritual
resources are available for training a young believer for
Christian service. Preparing oneself for His service lies in
faithfulness towards the local assembly and participation in all
its activities. Training is also essential in one's private life, which
should be characterized by an orderly and disciplined manner.
Much time should be spent in private prayer and reading and
studying the Bible, for it is vital to get a good grasp of the truth
of Scripture. This type of training goes hand-in-hand with being
a soul-winner in reaching out to the unsaved. In this whole
endeavour, younger Christians in particular should learn with a
humble spirit from men of experience in the faith, as seen in the

Acts of the Apostles. These are the Scriptural ingredients for becoming a missionary!

In September 1952 I left Holland and lived for three years in Germany. Looking back over these years I received much blessing, as I was privileged to listen to the ministry of godly men like Mr. Erich Sauer, who became well-known because of his books, translated into many languages. What a deep impression this brother made upon my life! Not only because of his ability to expound the Word of God, but even more so, because of his humble Christian character. It was during this time that I prayed to the Lord for guidance as to where to serve Him. Since God's field is the whole world, which corner of the great vineyard was meant to be my place?

Corrie ten Boom

In practising faith in its simplicity, Corrie ten Boom was an inspiring example to me. Soon after my conversion I got to know her and I was privileged to call her 'Tante Corrie'. My life was influenced by Aunt Corrie's simple but powerful testimony. The ten Boom family used to live in Haarlem, a place 20 miles (30 km.) outside of Amsterdam. Mr. ten Boom repaired watches and clocks and owned a nice store in a good location. Corrie also became a watch-maker, the first woman in Holland to be qualified for this kind of work. It was quite noisy in the shop with all the different clocks striking more or less at the same time and ticking the time away. But during the war things changed drastically in these peaceful surroundings. The house of the ten Boom family had become a haven of refuge. Father Casper and his two daughters, Betsie and Corrie, risked their lives, as the clock-repair shop became a centre of underground activity. From their place in town the refugees were smuggled to a safer place in rural areas. In this manner the ten Boom family was instrumental in sparing the lives of hundreds of people! It took tremendous courage to provide a hiding place for Jews. How true were the words of those days: 'The walls have ears...', when tragedy hit this family because of treachery. On the last day of February of 1944 German soldiers suddenly forced entry into the house. Four Jews and two resistance fighters were able to reach the secret hiding place in Corrie's bedroom just in time, and though the Germans searched the whole house thoroughly they did not find them. For the others it was too late, and they were arrested, nearly 30 in all. Also six members of the ten Boom family were put into prison and deported to a concentration camp in Ravensbrueck, Germany. This was a death camp and what a grieving experiencing for Tante Corrie to see so many people die! But at the same time what a blessing to have Tante Corrie there, because she was instrumental in guiding desperate people to the living Saviour. Corrie's sister Betsie died in this concentration camp, while other members of the family met their death in prison in Holland. What a prayer of Corrie ten Boom, when she came out of Ravensbrueck alive! "Lord, I thank Thee that it was Thy perfect will for me to be there. I know that Thou hast used Betsie and me to lead many people who faced a cruel death to Thee, and that was worth all our sufferings, even Betsie's death!"

When Corrie ten Boom returned to Holland, she promised herself: "I'll go anywhere God will send me, but never again to Germany". But it happened that she was spoken to by the powerful Word of God: "Love your enemies, bless them that curse you, do good to them that hate you, and pray for them who despitefully use you, and persecute you" (Matthew 5:44). These were the very words which brought a complete change of mind, and she became an ambassador of the Lord Jesus Christ, as the Lord called her to witness of the love of God. Her ministry was especially aimed at prisoners, and as she travelled around the world, first of all to Germany(!), she was instrumental in the salvation of many people. Tante Corrie visited 64 countries and keeping to the slogan: "To win souls for Christ is the greatest work which ever could be done here on earth", she called herself a 'Tramp for the Lord'. Her message was so simple, but at the same time so powerful: "Jesus is Victor"! When Tante Corrie went to be with the Lord on April 15, 1983, she had accomplished much for the Lord Jesus Christ, leaving behind a powerful testimony by which so many, myself included, were richly blessed and encouraged.

The Lord used Tante Corrie to speak to my heart. While she was giving report meetings about her extensive journeys, God drew my attention to a country in the Far East—Japan. During the war this country fought with Holland over the Dutch East-

My fiancee, Gerda Hengeveld

Corrie ten Boom

Indies. The Dutch fleet was engaged with the Japanese in the
Sea of Java where nearly all the Dutch ships were lost. Then to
think about the cruelty done to Dutch citizens, especially to
those who worked on the Burma railroad project. Every yard of
railway cost the lives of so many people. "Is this the country the
Lord is leading me to?" Still hesitant as I was, I asked for the
Lord's clear guidance. The Lord spoke to me through His Word
in reading Jeremiah 31:10, "Hear the Word of the Lord, O ye
nations, and declare it in the isles afar off." These words
impressed my heart, since Japan is a country of islands. An
additional confirmation of the Lord's call would be the consent
of the elders of the home assembly. It is a Scriptural principle
that concerning the Lord's work the authority remains in the
local assembly. Saul and Barnabas, who went out from the
assembly at Antioch, were never 'free-lance' missionaries, but
they went out as servants of the Lord 'commended to the grace
of God for the work to which they were called'.

When I approached the elders of my home assembly I found
them very willing to stand behind me. All believers of
assemblies in Holland were quite excited about it, since I would
be the first missionary going out from Dutch assemblies. In the
years after the war it was difficult to transfer money out of the
country, and to help in this matter some responsible brethren
took the initiative to establish a fund. According to the
Scriptural pattern, a fund has a right to exist as long as it fulfills
a ministry similar to the 'Epaphroditus service' (Phil.4:18). A
fund can only serve as an agent to forward gifts as they are
received from the donors. Unfortunately, after I had left for
Japan, things in Holland did not develop according to this
pattern, and it was not long before this fund was changed into a
'Mission Society'. The whole endeavour was a complete new
undertaking for the Dutch assemblies and due to a lack of
constructive and convincing teaching of New Testament
principles, the influence of human leadership became inevitable.

An Important Matter

Before I left for Japan I prayed for the solution of a very
important private and personal matter. I was drawn to a girl
from a nearby assembly. I loved her not only because she was
attractive, but also for her good Christian character. I wrote her

a short letter, in which I asked her whether she was willing to meet me and have a talk together. I got an affirmative answer and on a beautiful spring day in April 1955 we met and went for a walk in a nearby park. After talking about several things, I took the courage to speak about a most important matter. I told Gerda about my feelings towards her, but I fully realized the consequences of a positive answer. She would have to leave parents, relatives, friends, her job and all that was dear to her. I thought about this far-reaching effect and therefore I did not ask for an answer right away. "Pray about it and give me your answer later, let's say after six months", was my wise and thoughtful suggestion, but Gerda assured me that she did not need half a year for prayer. I quickly cut the time in half, but she told me that she did not need three months either. "What about some weeks", I still dared to utter. "No," she said, "I have prayed already for a few years for this moment to come and since I love you I am prepared to marry you, as I feel called by the Lord to serve Him in the capacity of a missionary's wife." I really was amazed! We thanked the Lord that He had already done the work of preparation, without either party's knowledge. We felt that this was guidance of the Lord! Happily we strolled back to her house where I left her and returned home on my bicycle—a very happy man indeed!

In those days money was very scarce, and it was some time until funds were sufficient for a ticket for one person to Japan. At that time, travelling by plane was too expensive. Before leaving my native soil there was a farewell meeting, and I was encouraged by the words spoken. I still hear the words of an old brother, saying, "If your going to Japan will result in the salvation of even one soul, it is worthwhile to follow the orders of the Master". In 1955 I left Holland and said good-bye to my parents, relatives and the believers in the assemblies. Some of them I never met again, but I still do remember them with gratitude in my heart. My father was taken by a sudden heart attack, so I never met him again, but I know that he was thankful to have a son in the Lord's work. During those sad moments of leaving loved ones behind, I fully realized that the call of the Lord is not just an exciting adventure, but it means to be a living sacrifice laid upon the altar (Rom. 12:1). Being assured of the call, the Lord gave me strength to leave all and everything behind for the sake of the Gospel. "So likewise, whosoever he is of you that forsaketh not all that he hath, cannot be my disciple" (Luke 14:33). But what is my devotion to God compared with the sacrifice of the Lord Jesus, who gave Himself for me?

> Thy life was given for me,
>   Thy blood, O Lord, was shed
> That I might ransomed be,
>   And quickened from the dead;
> Thy life was given for me;
>   What have I given for Thee?
> (Believers Hymn Book—No.458)

CHAPTER FIVE

By Freighter to Japan

After a train journey through Germany and Switzerland I arrived at Genoa where I met my German friend Johannes, who was also going out as a missionary to Japan. On the Dutch freighter *Abbekerk* there was accommodation for only 12 passengers. I shared a nice cabin with Johannes, and we enjoyed our sea journey very much. On its 45-day journey the ship called at places like Port Saïd in Egypt, Djibouti in Africa, Bombay in India, Colombo in Ceylon (now Sri Lanka), Penang and Port Swattenham in Malaysia, Singapore, Hong Kong, Manilla and even Shanghai in Red China. Wherever possible, we contacted missionaries or native Christians and experienced refreshing times of fellowship. The stopover in Communist China was for only three days, and soldiers of the Red Guard, who took temporary control of the ship, spoke to us a lot about the good things of 'New China'. We tried to draw their attention to the necessity of the new birth in order to enter the Kingdom of God, but as atheists they did not have an open ear for this kind of 'opium' of the people.

Nature's Wonders and Power

We were overwhelmed by the beauty of God's creation. While steaming through the Red Sea we got a glimpse of Mount Sinai, so we sat down together and read the corresponding chapters in the Bible where the Israelites crossed the Red Sea. In the Indian Ocean we were amazed to see the glowing phosphor fields in the water and also the flying fish and various other spectacular and impressive sights of nature. We had never seen a night sky so bright, so large, so beautiful, and as we glanced at the expanse of stars and planets while sailing over the oceans in Asia, we were struck with the magnitude of it all. "Lift up your eyes on high, and behold who has created these things, who bringeth out their host by number, He calleth them all by names by the greatness of His might; for He is strong in power" (Isa.40:26).

As the ship sailed along we were not only impressed by the beauty of nature, but also by its power. As we approached Japan our ship was caught in a violent tropical storm which had started during the night. We woke out of our sleep, as the ship was being tossed like a match box on the huge waves. During the whole journey I had not felt seasick, but now my stomach was churning. In the morning we went as usual to the dining room on the upper deck, but we could not believe our eyes at the sight of all the damage. The securely anchored chairs and tables had all broken loose and all the chinaware had been dashed to pieces on the floor. Coming into the lounge we saw that lamps and pieces of furniture had also been thrown around and badly damaged. Breakfast could not be served that morning, which was probably the best for upset stomachs. Since we could hardly walk we went back to our cabin, and while we lay on our beds the ship suddenly began to pitch violently from one side to the other to such an extent that, if we hadn't held on to the bed railings, we would have been thrown to the floor. The captain proceeded to make an announcement over the PA system that the ship had to change course in order to start a rescue operation. It was because of turning that the ship had become about broadside into the waves and been hurled about by the wild sea. The captain asked the passengers to go on deck and assist in the rescue operation. We put on our jackets and wrestled our way up to the ever shifting deck. When we looked over the railing we were shocked to see a small fishing vessel nearly submerged by the power of the typhoon. Part of the cabin was still above water, with six men holding on to it and another man clinging to the mast.

Our ship manoeuvred itself into position so that the fishing vessel would drift towards it. A huge wave suddenly smashed the little boat against the iron hull of the 10,000 ton freighter and it instantly splintered into thousands of pieces. There was literally nothing left that even looked like a boat! Before the submerged vessel was smashed against our freighter, the fishermen had to exercise split-second judgment to let go and dive off into the sea. The man clinging to the mast did not jump off in time and was instantly killed, but the others jumped clear safely and then began the struggle to keep themselves afloat.

A 45-day journey by cargo-ship to Japan

We were instructed to throw out all life buoys from the deck. Several of the men managed to grab one. The sailors of our ship pulled the first fisherman up and managed to get him on board and there was a sigh of relief. But there were still five to be rescued. The sailors were able to pull up another two, but the battle had become more difficult. Three fishermen were safe on deck, but the fate of the others still fighting the tremendous waves hung in the balance. We were so happy when two more managed to get on deck. Now there was only one fisherman left in the churning sea and the sailors did what they could to rescue him. One sailor even went down on a rope ladder, but was called back by the captain as the risk was extreme. Several times the remaining fisherman grasped a tethered preserver, but when he would be pulled halfway up to the deck, he would fall back into the rough sea because he had become too weak to hold on. At last the man was completely exhausted and we could see his desperation. It was not long before we helplessly watched as with his eyes wide open in terror and his arms outstretched he sank into the inky depths of the wild sea.

After an event like this, you can't help but think about eternity. The Bible clearly points to an eternal state after we take our last breath. What about the two lost fishermen? Each Christian has a debt towards his fellowman to be a witness of the Lord Jesus Christ. Because of the language barrier we could not convey even one word to the rescued Japanese fishermen. Yet, it was my first contact with Japanese people, and I was sure of the Lord's call just to be there for those in need of salvation.

As opportunities presented themselves throughout the sea voyage we held informal meetings on the crew deck. Johannes and I sang together with the guitar. There were always some sailors who came and listened to our testimonies. We also visited the sailors in their cabins to speak about eternal things. After the tragedy with the Japanese fishermen, the rough sailors paid much more attention to our words, and the tracts we distributed were eagerly read.

"It is better to go to the house of mourning, than go to the house of feasting; for that is the end of all men, and the living will lay it to his heart" (Eccl.7:2).

Entry into Japan

Finally the coastline of Japan came into view, the first port of call being Kobe. The freighter stopped there for four days and this gave us ample time to be with the missionaries and the Japanese Christians. The last part of our sea voyage was just one day from one Japanese port to another. When we reached our final destination of Yokohama, we were welcomed by some of the missionaries. That same evening we attended a missionary prayer meeting, where about thirty missionaries had come together for prayer. We were warmly welcomed to join their ranks in reaching souls for Christ.

The next day we left Tokyo for Karuizawa, a small town in the mountains of central Japan. It had been arranged for me to live there with three missionaries from Germany who were involved in language study. It was a bachelors' household and we took turns in putting a meal on the table. One of my friends sometimes took it very easy and 'prepared' a meal which consisted of peanuts and apples, because this needed no cooking. The pans we used were also very simply made. I remember entering the room with a nicely prepared meal of hot porridge for our breakfast, when suddenly the handle came off and the porridge spilt all over the floor. After this I thought it would be better to follow the example of my friend and that morning our meal consisted of peanuts and apples.

I was thankful for meeting my missionary-friends, they encouraged me to get a good start in learning the language. Their advice was forwarded like this: "For the time being, forget about being a missionary. See yourself as a student eager to learn a most difficult language". The first missionaries we had met in Kobe were Mr. and Mrs. Thomas Hay, originally from England, but later commended from Canadian assemblies, and Mr. and Mrs. Albert Dexter from England. The Hays, commended in 1930, had been missionaries in Japan and Formosa (Taiwan) before the war. The Lord had used them in different areas to open up assembly work but they had first of all settled in Kobe while learning Japanese. The Dexters were originally commended to the Lord's work in China. After China was overrun by the Communists in 1948 the missionaries were expelled. Quite a number of these missionaries found a new field of labour in Japan, among them also the Lowers, the Bishops and Miss Brixton, all from England, and the Beckons from the United States. The Dexters came to Japan in 1951 and laboured for many years in the Kobe area. Among the Japanese Christians in the assembly there was an outstanding brother by the name of Dr. Ishihama, who was a dentist and spoke English fluently. I recall the wonderful times of fellowship with this brother, who showed a zealous dedication in his life to the Lord. During the war Dr. Ishihama was imprisoned for preaching at an open-air meeting against the 'Sun Goddess', the chief deity of Shintoism. It was a most dangerous time for the testimony of the three existing assemblies in Tokyo, Kobe and Osaka. Spies were planted in the meetings, the leading brethren were arrested, and several of them spent all of the war years in prison until Japan's surrender on August 15, 1945.

Another pre-war missionary was Mr. R.J. Wright from Northern Ireland, who came to Japan in 1931. By the outbreak of the war he was interned at Yokohama. Fortunately, a year later he was repatriated in a prisoner exchange program. Another missionary from Northern Ireland, Mr. John Hewitt, who had come to Japan in 1938 was put in a concentration camp, where he died in 1942 because of ill-treatment. His death was the only war-time martyrdom recorded among missionaries in

Japan. When Mr. R.J. Wright was released from prison and left Yokohama by ship, he carried an urn containing the ashes of John Hewitt and John's Bible with him back to Ireland.

In recent years I have been at his graveside at Kilmore and I have thanked the Lord for His servant who was faithful unto death. On his gravestone the words are written:

John Alexander Hewitt
Missionary, who died in Japan 7th April 1942
And his ashes are interred here
"FAITHFUL UNTO DEATH"

During the war there existed a rude military Shinto regime, under which the testimony of the few assemblies was virtually broken up. After the war these assemblies were soon re-established and since 1948 there has been an influx of missionaries with the result that many more assemblies were started.

My Fiancee's Arrival and Our Wedding

My fiancee, Gerda, left Holland about one year later. The voyage lasted 55 days and since she was susceptible to seasickness, she had many a rough day. Gerda was to disembark in the port of Kobe where I met her. I had travelled to Kobe already two weeks ahead of time, not only to be in time to meet my bride-to-be, but also to help in on-going tent meetings. These meetings were held at a good location in the city, and every night a good number of unsaved heard the Gospel. I could not yet preach in Japanese, but was very happy to help in invitation work. At that time, tent meetings were still quite popular, and it was an effective method to invite people to listen to the Gospel. In later years, when Japan became a more prosperous country, tent meetings became less attractive, and today it is better to conduct meetings in more comfortable air-conditioned halls. When at last the day of Gerda's arrival came, Mr. and Mrs. Hay joined me to welcome her. It was thrilling to watch the big ship steam into the harbour, and as soon as I saw Gerda standing on deck, I began to snap pictures with my camera. After the ship docked I was one of the first to go on board in order to meet my sweetheart. Mr. and Mrs. Hay

The five Japanese fishermen rescued in a typhoon

Our first Sunday spent at Kobe

followed a short time after with great courtesy and consideration. After our brief initial meeting, I took even more pictures of my beautiful girl. By then it dawned on me that I must have taken at least 50 pictures on a film of supposedly 36. I checked the camera and discovered that it had no film in it. Excitement can do that to you!

Soon we left for Tokyo, and from there continued our journey to Takasaki, since that was the place where Gerda would live to make a start in the Japanese language. How good to receive help and hospitality from other missionaries. First Gerda enjoyed hospitality from a German couple, Mr. and Mrs. Stoecker, and then from Mr. and Mrs. Leonard and Agnes Mullan from Northern Ireland. The Mullans have always meant a lot to us, as they were missionaries not only to the Japanese, but in many ways also to other missionaries. While they were in Japan from 1952 till 1987, the Lord granted much blessing upon their labours for Him. Gerda and I lived about 80 miles (120 km.) apart and since we both were fully occupied with our studies, we met each other only twice a month. For the sake of the Lord's work, we felt that our priority should not be personal matters.

On one occasion I was on my way to Takasaki by train. It was already quite late, but it seemed that I would make it to the Mullan's house by around eleven o'clock in the evening. I was probably thinking too much about Gerda and in my excitement I got off one station too early, and there I was standing in the cold and windy weather, waiting another two hours for the next train. I was really embarrassed to arrive so late, but the Mullans showed pity on me and let me in.

Our wedding day was in May 1957. It was a simple but joyful wedding in the presence of many guests, missionaries from all over Japan and Japanese Christians. We were helped by some of the missionaries to arrange the details for our wedding. Goodies were baked, the wedding hall was decorated, and many more things were accomplished to make it an unforgettable day for us. Although far from all our relatives in Holland, we felt the impact of the words of the Lord Jesus more than ever: "So likewise, whosoever he is of you that forsaketh not all that he hath, cannot be my disciple" (Luke 14:33). The Lord united us in marriage for the great purpose of serving Him together and we raised our voices of thanksgiving to Him!

CHAPTER SIX
How we got to know Japan

The Country and its People

The name, Japan, derives from the Chinese, pronounced as *Jih-pen*, but the Japanese pronunciation of the characters is *Nippon*, the name written on postal stamps. The meaning of the two symbols is 'sun' and 'basis', together it stands for 'rising sun'. Japan is a country of islands—the four main islands are: Hokkaido, Honshu, Shikoku and Kyushu and there are many smaller ones. These islands form the summit of an underwater volcanic mountain range. There are some active volcanoes, and often the country is plagued by seismic events and eruptions. Some of the earthquakes are quite heavy, causing casualties and damage. Another danger for the peaceful Japanese islands are the typhoons or hurricanes that sweep in from the Pacific Ocean, taking a heavy toll in human lives and causing a lot of damage to property.

The country has always been protected from invaders by the sea. In all of its recorded history, Japan never lost a war till the Second World War. The people take much pride in their history and cultural heritage. Japan is a beautiful country with rice paddies nearly all over the country, levelled and terraced, and with neat tea plantations and an abundance of fruit trees and vineyards. Japan as a whole has a temperate climate, but in the south the weather is sub-tropical. There is plentiful rain, mainly occurring in the rainy season from the middle of June till the middle of July. Lush vegetation makes the Japanese islands a beautiful part of the world.

Because of its geographical situation, this island nation has always been one of the most traditional and isolated countries in the world. It is a little smaller than the State of California, but accommodates more than 125,000,000 people. Since 70% of the country consists of mountains, all these people live on only 30% of its available land, mostly in the plains along the coastline. In the plains, population density reaches nearly 4,000 people per square mile, as compared to The Netherlands—also a flat country—where there are about 900 inhabitants per square mile. The Kanto Plain where Tokyo is located is a comparatively small area of land, yet it is inhabited by 40 million people. Land prices are extremely high, to the extent that nowadays it is not possible to buy a house in the Tokyo area, no matter how small or old the house may be, for less than one million dollars. Because of the tremendous price of building lots, houses are cramped together with very little space in between. Japan does not have the palatial residences of America or Europe. There are some, but for the average Japanese his life is still on the 'tatami' in small dwellings. The *tatami* are the Japanese pressed straw mats, laid like wall-to-wall carpet. The measurement of a *tatami* is 72 x 36 inches (180 x 90 cm). All rooms are measured by the number of *tatami* mats. A room could be a three-mat, a four-and-a-half-mat, a six-mat, an eight-mat room or even larger with more *tatami* mats. Many apartments have just two small rooms. Especially in the outskirts of big cities rows of apartment buildings are cities in themselves.

Before the war Japan was an agricultural country, but after 1945 technology and industry developed rapidly, resulting in quality consumer products being exported world-wide. Though Japan has no major natural resources of itself, and therefore all raw materials like crude oil must be imported, it has become one of the strongest industrial giants of the world.

When a visitor arrives in Japan the first overwhelming impression is the crowds of people, and they all seem to look alike. In the beginning we could not distinguish between Mr. Sano and Mr. Kobayashi, as both had black hair and dark brown almond shaped eyes. Anthropologists claim that the Japanese are a Mongolian race, like the Chinese and Koreans. These people also have black hair, dark brown and almond shaped eyes because of a fold of skin in the upper eyelid that reaches down over the inner corner of the eye. It is interesting to notice that for identification in Japan there is never any mention of eye or hair colour.

The Japanese are steady and loyal in their work, and it is their character to be submissive to the tradition and life-style of their society. A Japanese does not see himself as an individual in society, but as one belonging to the *dantai* (the group). As one big family, their society is based upon collective thinking and collective actions. Japan has never produced great personalities with a strong influence or men who became world-famous e.g. Lincoln in the U.S.A., Churchill in England or Gandhi in India.

Contact with the West

The first contact with the Western world was established in 1543 when Portuguese ships entered the port of Tanegashima in the South. At that time firearms were also introduced; and in 1571 the port of Nagasaki was opened to Portuguese traders. Merchant vessels also carried Catholic missionaries over to Japan. However, about 15 years later there was an imperial decree ordering the expulsion of the missionaries and the confiscation of all firearms. In 1609 Dutch traders were able to enter Japan and they established a factory on the little island of Hirado. It was not long before the Portuguese traders were expelled and only the Dutch were granted a favourable trade agreement. In 1641 these traders were transferred from Hirado to Deshima in Nagasaki harbour. We have been in this area a few times and have seen the sloping lanes built by the Dutch and the construction styles which also have distinct traces of Dutch architecture. For many years Holland was favoured as the only Western nation which was allowed to trade with Japan. In fact the Dutch-Japanese relationship covers a period of nearly 400 years. In recent years a complete 'Dutch town' has been built on the southern island of Kyushu near the port of Nagasaki. There, famous buildings from Holland like the Queen's palace in the Hague, the Dam Square in Amsterdam and the Dom Cathedral in Utrecht are replicated to scale, and the workmanship is outstanding. The 'Dutch Town' draws a lot of Japanese tourists. It was not till the middle of the nineteenth century that Japan opened itself to other nations. In 1853 Commodore Matthew C. Perry arrived from America at the port of Uraga and this resulted in a political and commercial treaty between Japan and the United States.

Customs

Since Japan's staple food is rice and fish, it is common to eat rice three times a day. For a westerner every meal may look the same, and he may get the impression that they eat rice with fish every day and maybe on special days fish with rice! However, there are many side-dishes, so there is quite a variety in the meals. A Japanese dish is first of all designed as a visual presentation and then as one of taste. Usually three main colours are used in a dish, and foods and dishes are artistically arranged. Raw fish is abundant, of great variety, and quite delectable. Sometimes a bowl containing roasted grasshoppers is served. They are baked in oil and are crunchy. *Misoshiru* soup, made of dried fish and soybean paste, is an essential part of a Japanese meal. Many foreigners call it simply 'thumbsoup'. The reason for this is that the hostess who serves the meal usually holds the bowl in such a way that her thumb is literally in the hot soup. Nowadays the younger generation likes a western type of breakfast with cereal and toast. Fast-food restaurants like McDonald's hamburgers and Kentucky Fried Chicken are also popular with them. This contributes to a genetically taller and heavier race of Japanese.

To take a bath—to go into the *ofuro*, as the Japanese say—is quite a ritual in itself. The Japanese *ofuro* is completely different from the Western style bath. It is small and deep so that the occupant can sit in hot, steaming water for an enjoyable relaxation. Nowadays the bathtub is filled with hot water from a boiler, but in earlier days a fire of wood underneath the tub heated the water. The dense steam coming out of the tub gives the impression that the water is boiling. With temperatures up to 115 Fahrenheit (43 Centigrade) a foreigner would come out of the tub looking like a red lobster! Every night the *ofuro* is prepared and everyone gets his turn in the proper order. First the father, then the sons, followed by the daughters and last of all mother takes her bath. With this type of bath, the first thing to do is to rinse yourself outside the bathtub. A long hot soak is next, sitting with bent knees in real hot water that reaches right up to the chin with only your head sticking out. There is never the discomfort of having knees and chest exposed like in our western baths. The next thing to do is to step out of the bathtub and sit on a little milkmaid stool to wash the body. After rinsing again, you remain even longer in the *ofuro* to relax. The Japanese say that one should never take a bath in a hurry.

Nowadays many houses have their own *ofuro*, and there are fewer public bath houses. Yet there are still many Japanese (about half the population) who prefer the public bath house, recognizable by its tall chimney from the furnace that is used to heat the water. Public bath houses are seen as a traditional social institution, a place to relax, where the news of the whole neighbourhood is passed on and where all kinds of things are discussed. It is sometimes even the venue for men to have business talks. Because of the volcanic activity Japan is blessed with many hot springs. In resort areas there are hot spring hotels, where the Japanese come to relax for two or three days. Not so far from where we lived there were many such places. A hike in the mountains could become quite an experience, as you find columns of steam emerging out of holes in the earth's crust. It does not take long to boil an egg in the tremendous hot steam.

Religion
Buddhism entered Japan in 533 AD and soon became the religion of the ruling class. The result was that the whole population was influenced by this new religion. The teaching of Buddhism emphasizes endurance and patience, and it is a component of Buddha's teaching not to show one's feelings in public. Even tragic news is often passed on with a smile. Once, a girl of about twenty told us of the death of her mother, laughing; she wanted to suppress her grief. Laughing is a way out when the Japanese feel bashful or embarrassed. A Japanese will never lose face and therefore he will not easily admit that he was wrong. A big smile settles the matter. However, a smile may hide a lot of inward pain and grief! Women are not supposed to show their teeth, so when they laugh it is expected that they put their hand in front of their mouth. Kissing is also an ' unacceptable expression of feelings in public, and consequently, 'kissing the bride' never occurs in a wedding ceremony. In fact the Japanese don't see kissing as a gesture of love and affection, but connect it with a sexual relationship.

In many ways their concept of love is very different from the western view. The Japanese feel that when two are brought together, love will be the inevitable outcome, and this makes the job of match-making a very interesting one. Of all marriages 70% are arranged either by parents, relatives, or a respected person like the company boss. In missionary work, it is also essential to be aware of this custom. These days the assemblies are quite well established, so that the Japanese brethren take an active role in acting as a 'go-between' to arrange marriages. However, in all fairness, the persons involved do have the right to decide for themselves, as they always have the last word as to whether they will accept the match or decline it. The persons who act as a 'go-between' proceed in stages, and at each juncture the young man and the young lady will be asked separately whether they wish to stop or to continue the process. An arranged marriage is not so much a romance, but is seen more as a partnership. It seems to be a safe method, since the divorce rate among arranged marriages in Japan is very low.

The native religion is Shintoism—this is a primitive pagan religion of nature-worship. Shinto means 'the way of the gods' and is strongly nationalistic. It teaches that the Japanese descended from the gods. Of the whole world first of all Japan was created from drops spilled out of heaven. According to Shinto teaching Japan could never lose a war, but since Japan was defeated in 1945 Shintoism obviously suffered a set back. However, that does not mean that the religion died out. To the contrary, it is still a tremendous force in modern Japanese society. Since Buddhism and Shintoism do not conflict with each other, the two religions have existed side by side throughout the centuries. The statistics say that 80% of the Japanese are Buddhists and 70% are Shintoists. In almost every non-Christian home one can find a Shinto godshelf and usually a very ornate Buddhist altar.

A little bit of influence from Christianity has created a trend among young people towards having a Western style wedding in a fancy Wedding Hall. Even in places like Hawaii and California there are Wedding Halls especially designated for weddings of Japanese couples. The life of a Japanese starts out with a Shinto birth ceremony, often a Christian-like wedding is performed, and it ends with a Buddhist funeral. To them there is nothing wrong with dividing their allegiance between Shintoism and Buddhism with a bit of Christianity inserted wherever it is convenient. According to Government statistics only 0.7% of the Japanese identify themselves with Christendom, in which are included Jehovah Witnesses, Mormons, etc.

Worship in front of a temple

Part of a temple

The first funeral we attended shocked us. A fancy hearse with a roof like a pagoda temple, black-lacquered sides with glass windows and covered with ornate reliefs of golden brass, is used to carry the body to the crematorium. Cremation is mandatory by law, since there is not sufficient room available to allocate a deceased person a piece of land of some square feet. The procedure of cremation is far more an involvement of family members in the East than it is in the West. Going down to the place where the furnaces are, those present watch the coffin being slid into the oven. The man in charge takes off his cap and there are a few moments of silence to pray to the deceased spirit. Then the mourners are requested to go into the waiting room till the ashes are brought in. The actual cremation process takes about 50 minutes. In big crematoria there are high tables to stand around. The family is guided to a certain table and the huge dustpan containing the ashes is put right in the middle. Then the ceremony of 'collecting the bones' begins, as each member of the family uses big chopsticks to pick up the small pieces of white burnt bones and put them into an urn, together with the leftover ashes. It is the custom to place the urn underneath a tombstone on the temple ground or nowadays also on a public cemetery in a ceremony conducted by a Buddhist priest.

Usually an assembly possesses its own plot in a cemetery and underneath a tombstone the urns are placed on a shelf. The funeral of a Christian in a heathen country like Japan is a great testimony of the victory of the Christian faith over death and the grave. "O death, where is thy sting? O grave, where is thy victory? But thanks be to God, which giveth us the victory through our Lord Jesus Christ" (1 Cor.15:55,57). What a great opportunity to preach the Gospel to the many unsaved who attend the funeral!

Service
The Japanese are a disciplined people. Even on the very crowded railway platforms, or bus stops, people line up in a considerate manner. During rush-hour there are stations which become so crowded that they will be closed until there is again space for people to enter. There are hundreds of stations in the city of Tokyo and the busiest is Shinjuku Station, which handles

two million people a day! Students are hired to serve as 'pushers' on the platforms, and it is their job to crowd more people into a train. Often when the pressurized doors are closed, and the train departs, jackets and coats stuck between the doors are left to flap like flags in the breeze. These electric trains often transport at more than 250 percent of capacity, and you have the feeling that it is more a matter of hanging than standing. Most foreigners are taller than the Japanese, and that is a distinct advantage in breathing. If you lift your foot, you can't put it down again, because that little piece of floor-space has been occupied by somebody else's foot; and you must be content to balance like a stork on one leg. The only way to re-occupy your territory is by first wedging the toe of your shoe onto the floor and gradually following it with the rest of your foot.

It is a country of great customer-service. At a gas station it is not unusual to have five attendants surround your car to fill it up, clean the windows and check your oil. In department stores and many shops a customer is welcomed by the word *Irasshaimase*. You will receive a warm welcome even in the elevator, where an attendant will tell you exactly what kind of goods are available on various floors. You are made to feel very special indeed.

Competition

In many ways Japan is a country of stress. The pace of life is fast and intense with hardly any time to relax. It is a noisy country, and train stations are especially so because of the blaring announcements over the loudspeakers and a one-minute buzzer announcing the departure of each train. In some restaurants the music is so loud that a normal conversation is hardly possible. Needless to say, among the Japanese there is a constant atmosphere of competition and survival of the fittest—already noticeable in kindergarten! If the parents manage to get their children into a superior kindergarten, it is more or less a guarantee for graduation from a better university. 'Tokyo University' is the most respected, and their graduates are certain to get the best jobs. Nearly all the government postings, including that of Prime Minister, are occupied by graduates from this university. Because of the competitive spirit, and the shame of losing face, many suicides occur, with most of the cases among young people aged 12 to 25. The most sorrowful example is a 'family suicide' where a father or mother is unable to bear the unbelievable pressure and kills himself or herself along with the entire family. Some of the most scenic locations, such as waterfalls or cliffs, are utilized by young people who have failed university entrance exams. Such failure ends their career hopes.

Because of success and recognition of status there is a lot of pride in Japanese society as a whole. Many men take overt pride in their company, and it is a common saying that a man has a greater love for his company than for his own wife—indeed it does appear that way! The men leave their offices at 7, 8 or even 9 p.m. and then endure a one to three hour ride in trains filled to over capacity. The company is often the place where a worker has security, as the firm takes good care of its employees in many areas, such as arranging a marriage, granting a personal loan, etc. All the extra hours put into the company are reflected in the year-end bonus as a token of the company's appreciation. This bonus can be equivalent to two or three months salary and for executives, up to half or even a full year's salary—all paid in cash! Lately however, as Japan has begun to experience some economic hardship, things have started to change.

Politeness

The Japanese are generally very polite and helpful. If you show uncertainty, for instance, as you might when you lose your way, a passerby may come up to you and ask, "Can I help you?" Politeness is the cornerstone of Japanese society. When we began to study the language our teacher told us the following: "Remember that the mouth and the heart are always two different things in Japan". In order to maintain politeness, it is expected and accepted to lie. How different from the Scriptural concept: "But let your communication be, Yea, yea; Nay, nay: for whatsoever is more than these cometh of evil" (Matt.5:37). It does not mean that there is no honesty in the Japanese society. On the contrary, it is still one of the safest countries in the world, with a very low crime rate. If, as a tourist, you forgot your suitcase on the platform of a very crowded railway station and come back an hour later to claim it, there is a 95% chance that you would find it still in the exact spot where you left it. In Western countries this is unthinkable. Because Japan is largely a cash society, it frequently happens that a tremendous amount of money is left behind in a taxi, bus or train. There is a good chance that the driver or the conductor would take the attache case or purse to a police station, for it is a custom in Japan that the finder gets at least 10% as a finder's fee.

There are a number of different levels of speech in the Japanese language. One could speak plain Japanese or polite Japanese. When addressing a person of higher social status, the polite speech is essential. The Emperor would never respond in the polite form of speech, but would use plain words in speaking to his subjects. There is a specific 'children's language', but also amongst men and women different words are used, as a 'women's language' and a 'men's language'. The language is cluttered with polite phrases which are not easy to remember, and in studying I had much difficulty in distinguishing them. At times I inadvertently used the wrong expression. Once when a shipment of personal belongings arrived from Europe and the truck driver kindly put it into the shed for me, I was supposed to have used a polite phrase to thank him for all the trouble he took. But instead I used the phrase to thank him for an elaborate meal. I noticed his perplexed look at the *hen na gaijin*—the 'funny foreigner'! Perhaps he thought that it was a shipment of food.

Discussions

In Japanese society the *sodan,* a discussion, holds a vital place. Without a thorough discussion nothing could ever be accomplished in this country. The reason is that a spirit of individualism does not exist; the thinking pattern, actions and behaviour of the Japanese are based upon collectivism. Therefore a decision is always the result of a *sodan* and so the final outcome becomes the decision of the family or of the company. The Japanese Government also reflects herd mentality as it is not the action of one minister that counts, but far more that of the political party as the result of a *sodan.* In the discussions, however, extra respect is shown for the elderly and experienced. The missionary work in Japan also depends on this essential to build the assembly on the basis of spiritual leadership and the ability to commune with all the believers. There must exist a sense of involvement by all the believers in every decision taken.

Discrimination

In many aspects there is still a feudal system in Japanese society. Though forbidden by law, discrimination is quite noticeable, and though there is progress for the better, women are still treated poorly compared to men. There is much freedom in a man's life. Often the evenings are spent with friends in the presence of hostesses in bars and clubs. Though women take 'second' place after men, in the family the wife is usually in full control of the finances to run the household well.

When referring to a foreigner the word *gaijin* is used. It has the meaning of being an outsider. Strangely enough Chinese, Koreans or other Asian people are never called *gaijin*. The word is used only for Caucasians. A lot is expressed in the use of this word. It means that you are foreign to Japanese society and culture. You may learn to speak Japanese perfectly and you may know a lot about their culture, yet you will never be able to enter into their world and be a real part of their society. This remains closed to foreigners, regardless of any mouthings to the contrary.

The elder son is traditionally obliged to take care of his parents till they die. His wife is not called the 'bride' of the groom, but the *yomeire,* which means a 'bride put into the family'. In former times, with large families, most had sons to carry on the family name. Today, with a birthrate of 1.7 per family the problem is solved in another ingenious way. When two girls are born into a family, one—preferably the oldest— marries a *hanamuko.* This means that her husband is received into the house of the girl's parents and treated as their son. He will take their name and thus continue the lineage of the family.

In view of the importance of having a son in those earlier days, we observed the concern among the Japanese over our growing family. The Lord blessed us with five children, each one of them accepted with great joy and thankfulness as a 'heritage from the Lord' (Psalm 127:3a). When our first child was born, a girl, the Japanese congratulated us sincerely, but when our second child was a girl as well, the congratulations did not seem as heart-felt.

*Our children: Linda, Marion, Carla, Monica and Robert
(Photograph of 1977)*

On the arrival of our third daughter we heard expressions like
zannen da, which means 'What a disappointment!' and when
our fourth daughter was born, the word *komatta* was heard,
which means something like 'Now we have a problem!' There
was of course never a disappointment on our side as we formed
a happy family with our four sweet girls: Linda, Marion, Carla
and Monica. But for the Japanese our situation must have
appeared to be beyond hope. When our fifth child came along,
and proved to be a boy, the Japanese were beside themselves
with joy, and congratulations were effusive. Upon the occasion
of Robert's birth, the Christians offered us a 'feastmeal', this
time not rice with fish, but rice with red beans, as a sign of good
fortune.

CHAPTER SEVEN
Participation in Missionary Work

Reaching out to the Japanese

Seeing the mass of people we were reminded how the Lord Jesus saw them—"And Jesus, when he came out, saw much people, and was moved with compassion toward them, because they were as sheep not having a shepherd: and he began to teach them many things" (Mark 6:34). The Lord knew what compassion was. As He beheld the city of Jerusalem, the representation of the nation of Israel, He wept over her—tears as a display of His love for the nation (Luke 19:41). When He wept at Bethany, where Lazarus had died, the Jews said: "Behold how He loved him!" There, tears were shed as a display of love for an individual (John 11:35). May we have compassion and a love for the people as the Lord manifested. Only with a burden laid upon our hearts to see precious souls saved, can the great task be undertaken. What a tremendous privilege to make Christ known to a people living in darkness!

Often a Japanese would approach us with the following words: "Why did you come to Japan? Are you here to bring us a new religion? We have our own religions and we don't need more." They indeed have their own religions: Shintoism and Buddhism with all its different sects. But how good to be able to give the answer: "We are here not to bring you a new religion, but to present to you the living Saviour. Our preaching does not concern the proclamation of a religion, but it concerns the preaching of 'Christ, and Him crucified' (1 Cor.1:23). Our faith has nothing to do with a religion, but has everything to do with the living Saviour."

To reach the Japanese with the Gospel it is essential to speak their language. The Japanese language is not built up of the 26 letters of the alphabet. There is a kind of Japanese 'alphabet', consisting of 48 phonetic symbols. There are no Roman letters, like our 'A-B-C's', it is more a picture language. These symbols

71

are called *kanji* and there are at least 50,000 of them. Many of these *kanji* come from China, but over the centuries they have changed. These *kanji* have two totally different pronunciations, one called the Chinese and the other the Japanese pronunciation. Both are used in colloquial Japanese, but the Chinese pronunciation occurs mostly in the use of a combination of two symbols.

Most missionaries in the early days followed the course of the Naganuma Japanese Language School. The standard for missionaries was a study of four books, which usually took two years. I gave myself entirely to this task, using about eight hours a day for my studies. No effort is too much for the sake of the Gospel. With God's help I learned to speak, to read and to write this difficult language. But it was not without strain. I remember that I had times when in my dreams these Japanese symbols came flying to me from all directions.

During the first year of language study I lived in Karuizawa, a summer resort in the mountains of central Japan at a 3,000 feet (1,000 meters) elevation. The little house would serve its purpose as a summer cottage, but not as a residence during the extremely cold winters. Built of very light materials, it was not possible to maintain a stable temperature in the house. The walls were made of thin plywood with an open space between, which contained no insulation. The temperatures easily dropped to minus 25 degrees Celsius, and living there year-round through the winter was not a pleasant experience. Water pipes froze regularly, so that there were times when the bath and toilet could not be used.

The nearest assembly was located at the foot of the mountains, and in order to get there we boarded a train pulled by 4 locomotives which went through a myriad of tunnels. Once I made the same trip on the back seat of a motor scooter belonging to a German missionary over a suicidal gravel road with 189 dangerous curves close to deep ravines—it was not a trip to be repeated!

My first practical participation in a Japanese meeting was a short comment about a Bible verse and although I had spent a lot of time preparing my message, I only managed to speak for about five minutes! It would have been easier if the gift of tongues were still available today, but since it is clear from Scriptures that 'sign gifts' were only temporary in their purpose

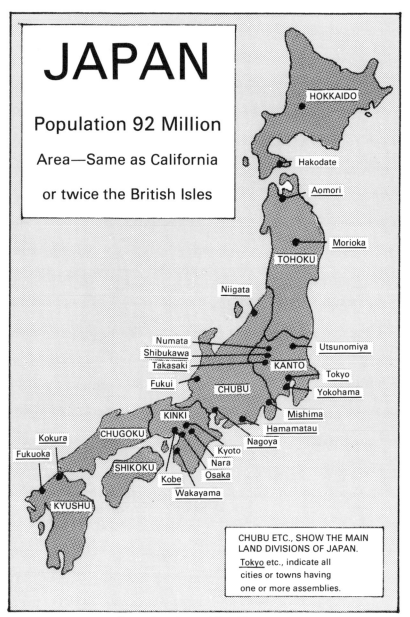

JAPAN

Population 92 Million

Area—Same as California

or twice the British Isles

HOKKAIDO

Hakodate

Aomori

Morioka

TOHOKU

Niigata

Numata
Shibukawa
Takasaki
Utsunomiya
KANTO
Tokyo
Fukui
CHUBU
Yokohama

KINKI
Mishima
Hamamatau
Kokura
CHUGOKU
Nagoya
Fukuoka
Kyoto
Nara
SHIKOKU
Osaka
Kobe
Wakayama
KYUSHU

CHUBU ETC., SHOW THE MAIN
LAND DIVISIONS OF JAPAN.
Tokyo etc., indicate all
cities or towns having
one or more assemblies.

Expansion of assemblies till 1959

and operation, we had to go through the struggle of mastering one of the most difficult languages in the world. But what a joy to be able to reach the people with the Gospel in their own language!

Since living in the mountains at Karuizawa did not afford much opportunity to practise what we had learned, my friend Johannes and I decided to move to Tokyo for our second year of language study. In those days there were assemblies in Tokyo which conducted nightly meetings in their halls and open-air meetings in front of nearby stations. This gave ample opportunity to get a good start in using our language ability. Living among the Japanese we were fully exposed to both the language and the Japanese culture. We enjoyed our new house very much. When I married in May 1957 my German friend was willing to move out to make this little house available for the newly weds. Gerda and I found happy fellowship in an assembly established a few years earlier by Mr. Adrian Presson, an American missionary who worked in Japan from 1952 till 1985. While he and his wife were on furlough for about 18 months, we found that the time spent with this little assembly at Higashi-Kitazawa was a profitable preparation for the next step in commencing a pioneering work.

Pioneer Work

Assembly missionaries in Japan have come from several different countries but there has never been any distinction made because of nationality. Among these missionaries, Mr. W.J. Wright has been in many ways a spiritual help to us. With a tremendous zeal for spreading the Gospel, Bobbie—as we used to call him—had a great vision for the Lord's work in Japan. He always spoke about 'occupying' the big cities on the main island Honshu. Before deciding on a place to start a pioneering work it was important to make enquiries about the particular area. I made some trips to different areas, even as far as Kyushu in the south. Some of the missionaries and Japanese Christians have travelled with me from time to time. On one occasion Mr. Wright joined me and gave me valuable advice. His vision has since been realized in a most remarkable way, as brethren, Japanese and foreign, have moved to the main centres all over the island of Honshu, where in due time assemblies have been

"Japan-Missionary" in the official Japanese dress for men

established. In this chain of assemblies we opened up a new work in the province of Tochigi. After much prayer and orientation we decided to move to the city of Utsunomiva, the capital of the Tochigi Province.

To go 'house hunting' was not always an easy job in Japan. It was a sad thing to experience sometimes a refusal because of being a *gaijin* (foreigner). However, there were also kind people willing to rent their house to us. Our desire was to rent a house in a strategic location close to the main street, suitable for starting a new work. The house itself was a primitive, old dwelling with low ceilings. When I stood on my toes, my head touched the ceiling. I had therefore to be careful not to lift the children above my head.

It was not difficult to furnish our house, since we did not as yet own much. As a wedding present we received from the missionaries a rattan set of three chairs. We added a small matching coffee table. An old wooden crate served as a 'sideboard'. With a cloth and a few ornaments on top it looked quite attractive. Throughout the years we have learned to be content with whatever house we lived in. The most important thing is to make a house a home where love, happiness and security dwells, and where guests find a warm welcome. The old house had no yard at all and in front was a narrow sand path on a five foot wide muddy creek. This river was used for sewage, so the smell was terrible. Water rats found an easy entrance through the open sewage pipes into our kitchen. Since the river was not fenced off, our landlady warned us to keep an eye on the children when they were outside. The Japanese toilet the *obenjo* consisted of a hole in the floor and the container underneath the house was emptied once a month. We remember the times when a man, holding a scoop in his hand and two buckets on a crossbeam over his shoulder, did the undesirable job of 'toilet cleaning'. In later years a truck with a huge vacuum tank was used to suck out the contents. Since the house had only one entrance—the front door—the dirty vacuum hose wound its way through the little entrance hall and the kitchen into the *obenjo*. Not very hygienic, to say the least!

The first tropical rain storm of the season changed the baby crib into a mini swimming pool, as water seeped from the ceiling into the crib. Our newborn baby, Marion, was not too

Living at Karuizawa together with three German missionaries

appreciative and her cries woke us up. An old house draws insects, especially during the rainy season. The *abura-mushi*, an ugly kind of cockroach, and the 'jumping spider', which can jump about 10 feet, were really awful. These insects eat both food and clothes, and to make matters worse our house was next to a fish shop. We got to know first-hand how fish smells when it is drying in the sun, especially since the boxes of fish were put on the stone partition wall just beneath our living room window, attracting hundreds of flies of all sorts and sizes.

That old house though became a place of much blessing. First we had to get to know the neighbours and since it was the beginning of a pioneering work, there were not yet any Japanese Christians who could give us help in making contact with the people. We had two little children, so we strapped them on our backs in the same way as the Japanese people did, and went out to distribute tracts and invite people from a surrounding area. We also drew the people's attention with big posters announcing the meetings. We were regularly in the centre of the city, where there was no difficulty in giving out 500 tracts in half an hour. Every time we stood at this busy intersection, we faced the

Futara hill on which a huge Shinto temple was built. We were reminded of the apostle Paul in Athens, when he stood on Mars Hill, opposite the Acropolis, declaring unto the people bound in idolatry 'the unknown God', as the Creator of everything.

When we started the first meeting we were very encouraged with the turn-out. The meetings were held in Japanese style without any chairs or benches to sit on, but the *zabuton*, little cushions spread out on the Japanese straw mats, served their purpose well. The room was quite well filled and many probably came out of curiosity just to be in a foreigner's house, but we were thankful for the opportunity to make the Gospel known to these people anyway. There were not many foreigners living in Japan at that time and they were the objects of special curiosity, especially in rural areas. The Japanese gazed at the giants with their white skin, blond hair and blue eyes, to the extent that it even caused accidents. One time, a man riding a bicycle could not take his eyes off our little children, and so bumped into a parked car, fell, and hurt himself. We were so sorry for him!

Missionaries' children have always had a special attraction for the Japanese. Occasionally someone would come up to us and ask for just one blonde hair. We were not too keen on distributing the hairs of our children one by one as a kind of good-will offering! All dolls at that time in Japan had blonde hair and blue eyes and therefore the foreign children were seen as dolls. Because of the attraction to our children it was not difficult to run a good Sunday school. As a result of this work, children of a responsible age have accepted the Lord Jesus as their Saviour. Today they may have families of their own and live in different places all over Japan, but it remains a comfort to know that "the foundation of God standeth sure, having this seal, The Lord knoweth them that are His" (2 Tim.2:19).

It is a great blessing to have a faithful help-meet in the Lord's work. Gerda has always tried to put priorities right for the sake of the Gospel. In the Lord's work we have complemented each other. Gerda was able to reach women and children as I could never have done. With many classes in our own house and in other places, she had golden opportunities to tell about the Saviour's love towards sinners.

In our pioneering work we tried hard to win the confidence of the people. In the beginning we used the evening hours to pay a

First baptism in ice-cold water of a mountain river while it was snowing

A little wood-fire to warm up

visit to people, but soon we discovered that this was not suitable. It is not a normal Japanese custom to visit somebody in the evening except by invitation. Life in a Japanese home is so completely different from that in western countries. In Japan the men usually come home late from work and because of the custom to use much time in taking a bath, visits in the evenings were not appropriate.

Over many years we have used the Gospel tent. We put up the tent for the first time soon after our move to Utsunomiya and were impressed with the number of people attending. In preaching the Gospel during that tent campaign, God reached out to save and some answered the Gospel call. In later years a tent was not such a suitable method of reaching the people. Japan became a luxurious country and today people prefer to sit in a comfortable chair in an air-conditioned hall.

Another method for the Gospel outreach was by means of a Christian bookstore. We rented a store in the centre of the city and over many years it became a good place to contact people. We remain thankful for the ones who found the Saviour as a result of this work.

When Linda was about four or five years old, she said one night: "I feel so sorry for the Japanese who become Christians". "Why?" her Mum asked. "Well, you see, when they go to heaven they have to learn Dutch", so was her reasoning. We don't think the language in heaven will be Dutch or English, but we all will speak the same heavenly language in thanking the Lord Jesus for all He did for us on Calvary's cross.

First Fruits

We recall the first series of tent meetings, which resulted in the salvation of two girls 16 and 18 years old, and of Mrs. Kato, a woman 45 years of age. These souls have been faithful in following the Lord. Mrs. Kato went to be with the Lord some years ago, leaving a good testimony, especially among her children and grandchildren.

Japan, as elsewhere, has its share of shy people. One evening a 20-year-old young man came as far as the corner of our street with the intention of attending a Gospel meeting, but didn't have the courage to come closer to our house and went home again, feeling uneasy about it. A week later he tried again and

Our next door neighbour, a fishmonger at Utsunomiya

After a breaking of bread meeting

came as far as our house, but he still didn't have the courage to
knock on the door. Again he returned home. Another time he
came as far as our front door, even opening it, but then closed it
gently without stepping into the house. However, since this
young man was really longing to hear the message from the
Bible, he came the fourth time and finally succeeded in crossing
the threshold. As one of the first fruits of the work, he got
saved and is today a responsible brother in an assembly. God's
Word is true: "Ask, and it shall be given you; seek, and ye shall
find; knock, and it shall be opened unto you" (Matt.7:1). This
remains true as each servant of the Lord will have experienced
this miracle in the lives of many, who walked in the darkness of
pagan religions, but who saw the light. It takes a lot for a
Japanese to accept Christ as his Saviour, for it means that he
steps out of the tradition of a heathen society that is based upon
the principles of Buddhism and Shintoism. Some young
Christians who were unwilling to continue their participation in
the heathen customs and ceremonies were expelled from their
families. The house of the missionary is seen as the place of the
'foreign religion', and it happened that Japanese who came to
hear the Gospel were threatened by people of an extreme
Buddhist sect called *Soka-Gakkai*. Threats that their house would
be destroyed by fire, or that one of their children would die in an
accident were real.

    Today the attitude is more tolerant, but the very fact of being
a Christian is contrary to Japanese customs. The real problem
lies most of all in the ritual of ancestor worship. It is a
manifestation of Satan's power to keep people in the bondage of
darkness! Every day one of the family has to take care of the
offerings to the spirits of the ancestors. On the idolatrous
god-shelf a cup of rice, a cup of water and a *mikan*, a Japanese
mandarin orange are set out as daily offerings. Next, while
sitting on the *tatami* (the Japanese straw mats) and facing the
god-shelf, the act of worship is performed with bowed head and
prayer to the ancestors. This ritual is kept in every home, and
only when the head of the family becomes a Christian, will the
Shinto god-shelf and the Buddhist altar be removed from the
house. A Christian wife, son or daughter, however, could never
do this. When these expensive structures are abandoned by a
Christian man or a widow, it could happen that the idols will be

burnt in a bonfire by the Christians who gather for the occasion, singing hymns of victory of their faith in the Lord Jesus Christ.

A Christian living with an unsaved husband or unsaved parents is always subjected to a life full of trials and temptations. Every Christian will be faced with overcoming difficulties at school or at work because of the overpowering atmosphere of the heathen society around them. The result could easily mean being ostracized or even persecuted. But how wonderful that these Christians know to stand in the power of the risen Lord!

The preaching of the Gospel in a heathen nation is more a matter of explaining the Gospel than of preaching it. People don't have a concept of the one, true, and living God, or of the meaning of sin, so in the preaching there is a primary need to emphasize the existence of God as the one and only holy and righteous God. Once having explained the meaning of the Gospel, I spoke about the words of the Lord Jesus: "Father, forgive them, for they know not what they do" (Luke 23:24). That was the moment a young man of 16 got saved also as one of the first fruits in our pioneering work. It is encouraging to observe their dedication to the Lord, and some of these men, who were saved in their younger years are now pillars in the assembly.

Other Cities Reached

Our responsibility in the Lord's work was not limited to one place only. Many years ago, Dr. Tsukiyama, an eye doctor in Tokyo, conducted occasional Gospel meetings in the house of a Christian woman who lived less than 10 miles (15 km) from our house. This lady got saved in Tokyo just after the Second World War, but had moved back to her native place. Old brother Tsukiyama came to visit us and pleaded for our help. Soon a regular Gospel meeting was started at Kanuma and we recall the happy times of fellowship in the house of Mrs. Okamoto. These meetings bore fruit, and as a result, an assembly was established in 1972.

There was another place about 30 miles (45 km) from Utsunomiya to which our attention was drawn. We knew that a Christian lady was living there. Some years previously, Miss Yajima had been saved in Tokyo after having attended Gospel meetings in the little assembly at Higashi-Kitazawa. What a joy

it must have been for the believers there to see this precious soul
saved! Not so long after her conversion she returned to her
native place, Shimodate. Yajima San was an outstanding
Christian, witnessing of her Saviour. In doing so, she came into
contact with a lady 55 years old, who showed a keen interest in
the Gospel. Miss Yajima told her about a missionary who lived
not too far away, and one afternoon both came to visit us. After
Gerda served them Japanese green tea, the purpose of their visit
was relayed. "Would you be willing to come to my town and tell
us from that book, that Yajima San spoke to me about? Please
use my house for this purpose and I will invite other people as
well." Because of the bumpy gravel roads it took almost an hour
and a half to cover the short distance. When we entered the
house of Mrs Ichimura we found the room filled with people.
This scene reminded me of the apostle Peter being in the house
of Cornelius, where he found hearts prepared to listen to the
Word of God. "Now therefore are we all here present before
God, to hear all things that are commanded thee of God" (Acts
10:33b).

   The responsibility for the regular Gospel meetings at
Shimodate was shared with a few brethren from assemblies in
Tokyo, and as co-workers we have witnessed a work of God
develop. What a joy it was when first of all Mrs. Ichimura
professed to be saved! She had known a lot of hardship in her
life, especially after she lost her husband when she was 29 years
old and was left with two little children. She had searched for
the truth, to have peace, and had tried hard to find satisfaction
in the different heathen religions. She had spent a lot of money
in pursuit of happiness, but she never found it. In a last
desperate effort she became involved in the *Tenrikyo*, a
Buddhist sect, but during this time she met Miss Yajima. What a
change occurred after she was saved. Her thriving testimony
was clear evidence of it. She was a witness of the love of God to
all her relatives, friends and neighbours, and as a result we
experienced a time of great blessing as seeking souls attended
the Gospel meetings and many accepted the Lord Jesus Christ as
Saviour. Among them her daughter, daughter-in-law, older
sister, a niece and other relatives, along with some neighbours;
all women. Then we started to pray especially for the salvation

Yajima San a faithful witness at Shimodate

of men, but we had to wait a few years to see the first man saved,
later followed by others. What happy times of baptisms and of
wonderful fellowship around the Word of God and what a joy
when the opportune time came to see an assembly established!
It has been a remarkable guidance of the Lord that the three
established assemblies were able to build their own halls. We
realize that it is not the physical building itself which is
important. It revolves around the contents of the assembly, as
Christians coming together in the Name of the Lord Jesus
Christ. But in having their own premises to use, the Gospel was
allowed a free course in the different areas.

Leprosy Camp
I shall never forget my visit to a leper camp in the north of
Japan. The assembly in Aomori held regular Gospel meetings
there, and quite a number of lepers were saved. I was invited to
preach the Gospel to the lepers, and as we entered the building
by way of the backdoor we found ourselves right on the
platform. The lepers came through the front door into the hall,
sitting on Japanese straw mats. The platform was fenced off, so
that it was not possible to step down into the hall to be with the
lepers. Leprosy is a terrible disease which destroys the flesh and
nerves, especially of hands, feet, nose, mouth and ears. There
were about 60 lepers together in the hall, of which about 40
professed to be saved. The meeting started with singing and
when these people sang with great conviction the hymn "I'd
rather have Jesus than silver or gold" in Japanese, I could not
hold back my tears. These people were the outcasts of Japanese
society, but what a joy and happiness they expressed because of
knowing the Lord as Saviour! I had to ask myself: Can I
sing the words of this beautiful hymn without any reservation
in my heart? Is it not true that we sing the words of a hymn so
easily, but often don't extend its meaning to our lives or express
its reality? What a meeting we had with these dear Christians in
the leprosy camp where the Lord continued to do a mighty work
in saving more souls! Nowadays in Japan leprosy is rare but, of
those affected by it in past years, there will be a number in
heaven. They have trusted in the work of redemption
accomplished on Calvary's cross.

A baptism in a river

Speaking at a baptism

The Next Move

Having toiled in the Tochigi province for almost 14 years, we felt the Lord's guidance to undertake a move to a new place west of Tokyo. Our move brought us closer to the school, so our children could commute from home rather than stay at boarding school. It still took them one hour to travel by train, but we were so happy that our family was together again. Till then they had been five-day boarders at the 'Christian Academy in Japan' (CAJ), an American school for missionaries' children. Our help was needed in a newly established assembly. However, we still felt it necessary to provide ongoing help to the places where we had worked before, and this created quite a busy schedule of meetings. But the time came when we could leave these assemblies alone, believing His promise: "being confident of this very thing, that he which has begun a good work in you will perform it until the day of Jesus Christ" (Phil.1:6). In happy fellowship with Christians at Kawagoe we have seen His blessed hand upon the efforts to win precious souls for Christ. The assembly was built up, and with the special efforts of the Christians an apartment in a good location was obtained, which was renovated into a nice hall. In the expansion of the work the Japanese Christians have been a good example in their dedication to the Lord and in their faithfulness towards the assembly.

The Gospel Work in Korea

On occasion, I have had the privilege to preach the Gospel in the neighbouring country of South Korea where I was able to witness amazing results. In smaller towns just one poster to announce the meetings was sufficient to fill the hall to capacity. In rural areas the halls could not hold the crowd of people, and many were obliged to stand outside near open doors and windows, attentively listening to the Gospel message. I visited halls built in open fields, and wondered where the people would come from in such deserted places. There were only a few visible hamlets of 10 or 20 houses each, yet I was surprised to see people come from all directions, some of whom had walked for one or two hours. There was a hunger for God's Word and what an encouragement it was to see God's hand in saving precious souls! To my amazement there were not a few who accepted the Lord Jesus as Saviour.

House meeting at Kanuma

Sunday school class at Utsunomiya

One day, while I was in Korea, an American missionary took me for a ride until at length we came to a river where we parked the car. As we walked along the bank we saw children playing in the shallow river and I thought it would make a delightful picture, so I climbed up on the river bank to get a better shot. Suddenly the ground under my feet gave way and I plummeted down into a hole more than waist deep. I was in a very embarrassing and awkward situation, because I had fallen into a hole of human waste! When Korean toilets are emptied, the waste is simply poured into holes along the river or on open ground. What a sight! A missionary from Japan fallen into a deep cess-pool! I held my camera up, not for my friend to take a picture of me, but to spare it. In this situation the one thing that mattered was to get out of the hole as quickly as possible. Fortunately I got help and I went straight to the river to clean myself. Later I took a more thorough bath to get rid of the terrible smell. My clothes and shoes had to be thrown out, because the smell would remain, especially in leather shoes. It was poor comfort when I heard that other missionaries living in Korea had similar experiences.

Upon my return to Japan, at the first Monthly Missionary Prayer Meeting in Tokyo, I gave a report about the Lord's work in Korea. A missionary commented that in Japan a full year's effort is needed to see one soul saved. This was of course exaggerated, but it was a fact that progress in the Lord's work in Japan was much slower. There is a great difference between the Lord's work in Japan and in Korea, and it hinges upon the characteristics of the people. The Koreans are more emotional and therefore easier to reach, but on the other hand there seems to be a lack of stability. In this respect the Japanese are different, for even though the overall growth of the missionary work in Japan is much slower, the long-term results are that the assemblies are more stable.

The Dutch Community in Japan

While living in Japan as a missionary from Holland, opportunities also arose to be of help to the Dutch community as well. The Dutch Embassy requested my help to officiate at a remembrance ceremony on the fourth of May. On this day the war dead are remembered in the Netherlands and in places

The Sunday school treat at Utsunomiya

overseas. In Holland, at eight o'clock in the evening two minutes
of silence are observed and trains, buses and other traffic will
come to a complete stand-still. A remembrance ceremony is also
held at the cemetery of Allied forces, a little distance outside of
Yokohama. Since at that time I was the only non-Catholic
missionary from Holland, I could not refuse the invitation. It
gave me an opportunity to point to the responsibility of each
living soul. For the dead, we cannot change the eternal state, but
here on earth choices must be made—eternal bliss or eternal
condemnation. "He that believeth on the Son hath everlasting
life; and he that believeth not the Son shall not see life, but the
wrath of God abideth on him" (John 3:36).

As the 'chaplain' of the Dutch Embassy I had the privilege of
meeting ministers of the government and members of the Royal
family. At a reception for the present queen, Beatrix, I was
impressed by the intelligent questions she asked about our work
as missionaries in Japan.

Sayonara—Farewell

In following the Lord's guidance to give help to assemblies in
Holland, a final effort in a series of Gospel meetings in Japan was
crowned with the salvation of a number of souls. Seeing the
blessing, it became even more difficult to leave. Very
surprisingly we received an invitation from the Mayor to attend
a 'Sayonara reception' in the City Hall. Since Gerda held a
number of classes weekly for ladies and children, the Mayor
wanted to honour her, and at this reception he thanked Gerda
for the positive influence she had on the Japanese community.

It is with great gratitude we remember the testimonies of
many dear Japanese Christians who have passed on to be with
the Lord, and also of the many who are still there today
continuing in a steadfast walk before the Lord. When we arrived
in Japan in 1955 there were only 16 assemblies, but in 1986 we
counted 120 assemblies, spread out all over the isles of this
beautiful country. Before the First World War a few missionaries
worked under the most difficult circumstances of a Shinto
governmental system. After Japan's defeat in 1945 the door was
wide open for missionaries to enter because of a new law which
guaranteed freedom of religion. The post-war missionaries,
commended from assemblies of seven different countries, have

Gospel Hall near hamlet in Korea

Conference at Tokyo

toiled with tears to lay the foundation of the assembly work in different parts of Japan. We are very grateful to have had a part in that great work of the Lord. "They that sow in tears shall reap in joy. He that goeth forth and weepeth, bearing precious seed, shall doubtless come again with rejoicing, bringing his sheaves with him" (Psalm 126:5-6).

Japanese brethren have taken up the torch, and today we give credit to many faithful Japanese Christians who have a burning desire to make Christ known to their own people. The missionaries in Japan took to heart the charge given to Timothy by the great apostle: "And the things thou hast heard from me among many witnesses, the same commit thou to faithful men, who shall be able to teach others also" (2 Tim.2:2). Missionaries who went to Japan as pioneers, together with so many faithful Japanese Christians were, and are, 'the men of God', in bringing the light of the Gospel to a nation in need of the saving power of our Lord Jesus Christ!

During our life as missionaries in Japan we lived in eleven different houses, some very primitive, which served to remind us that we are 'strangers and pilgrims' in this world. Together we have served the best of Masters and have lacked for nothing in our lives as He faithfully supplied all our need. With the assurance and evidence of the Lord's hand upon us, we ended more than 30 years of service for the Lord in the 'land of the rising sun'. Eternity alone will manifest the real impact of all our efforts, done in weakness, but in fulfilment of the task laid upon us. What a manifestation of His abundant grace!

Reception in the Mayor's office to honour Gerda for her work among women and children, resulting in improved family relationships in Japanese homes

CHAPTER EIGHT

Organizational Difficulties

The path we walked as missionaries was not always easy, because missionary endeavour will ever be characterized by spiritual conflict: "For we wrestle not against flesh and blood, but against principalities, against powers, against the rulers of the darkness of this world, against spiritual wickedness in high places" (Eph.6:12)

Much could be said about the tremendous spiritual darkness in a modern and developed country like Japan. With its 'eight million gods' it remains a stronghold of the rulers of darkness. Wherever the work of the Lord is carried out, the experiences of victory and defeat, encouragement and discouragement run ever parallel, yet in all the circumstances the Lord stands true to His promise: "I will never leave thee, not forsake thee".

When difficulties on the mission field originate in the homeland, it means a hindrance in fulfilling the Lord's work. It is only fair to mention the organizational difficulties we met in our missionary endeavour, and it is with sadness in our heart that we recall these times of deep trials. Yet, in it all the Lord remained faithful. We have experienced His miraculous guidance because of the fulfilment of the words of Romans 8:28: "And we know that all things work together for good to them that love God, to them who are called according to His purpose". The Lord knows how to instruct and train His servants, and as Christians our whole life is spent in God's school, learning to serve and follow Him: "If any man serve me, let him follow me; and where I am, there shall also my servant be" (John 12:26).

Since the Lord is not physically walking any more here on earth, we cannot follow Him in the same manner as the disciples did. We follow Him by means of His Word. The Bible is the living Word of the living God and is the ultimate source of authority for life and practice. As we approach the subject of 'Organizational Difficulties', we wish it to be clear that our intention is not to minimize the zealous dedication of faithful brethren who have been a great blessing in our lives over many years. Nor is it our thought to exalt ourselves in spiritual pride over other believers who may have a different opinion. May we be kept from a carnal attitude towards our brethren! "And this commandment have we from Him, that he who loveth God love his brother also" (1 John 4:21).

Unwritten Rules

In the midst of the tremendous effort in adjusting to a new country with different habits and customs and trying to understand a people with an altogether different thought pattern and outlook on life, it grieved us that burdens were laid upon us from overseas. Even at the outset, during the time of language study, we were faced with solving fundamental issues concerning the Lord's guidance. It became obvious that the movements of missionaries were controlled by the Mission Institutions, established by men of assemblies in Holland and Germany. As time passed and decisions had to be made, it became evident that there were 'unwritten rules' to be observed. By choosing just to follow the Lord rather than the rules of men, we were accused of going our 'own' way and were put in a difficult position.

The first matter which caused disharmony was our move to Tokyo in 1956. Judging objectively, Tokyo was far more suited as a place for language study than a resort area up in the mountains. For my friend Johannes and I, the whole matter arose after we received a message from Mr. J.B. Currie, an Irish/Canadian missionary, working in Japan since 1948. He told us of a house belonging to a Japanese brother of the Fuchu assembly in Tokyo, which was available for an exceptionally reasonable rent. It had been used over many years as a home for missionaries in language study. At that time there were four assemblies in the Tokyo area which conducted many meetings during the week, providing ample opportunity to practise the language. Independent of our move, it just so happened that our language teacher had decided to move to Tokyo as well. Mr. Yamashita was an able teacher but, having only a few students and living in the remote mountain area of Karuizawa, he could not make ends meet. We were impressed to see the Lord's guidance in it all. We discovered, however, that this move did not meet with the approval of the brethren in the home land. The reason was that the summer house at Karuizawa was the property of the German Mission, and they felt that it should be used as a centre for language study.

Another point of friction surfaced when Gerda and I had decided on the date of our wedding. The reaction to setting the date was indeed upsetting. We were advised in letters to stick to the 'unwritten' rule of waiting a full year before getting married. This is the common practice of denominational Missions, and their rules were apparently taken as standard. The reason for this rule was for the missionary to be able to finish the basic course in Japanese. This normally requires a full year, but Gerda, because of her gift for languages, finished this course in less than six months. As we felt clear on the Lord's guidance we set the date and in May 1957 we were happily married. Although no relatives were present, the Japanese Christians and many co-workers in the Gospel were, and we enjoyed an unforgettable day! Mr. R.J. Wright performed the wedding ceremony, while Mr. Leonard Mullan spoke an encouraging word from the Scriptures about Aquila and Priscilla. This godly couple were a good example for our own missionary endeavour.

When the time came to decide on the place to start a pioneering work, we again faced a disturbing conflict. Apparently the area we had moved to as a result of much exercise in prayer was not the place to be in! It became evident that it was the intention of the Missions to set up a kind of 'German work', independent from missionaries of other nationalities. Although we were Dutch, in the homeland it was expected of us to work together with the German missionaries, and therefore we were supposed to have moved to an area on Japan's west coast where some of the German missionaries were already living. These missionaries, however, were involved in an extreme charismatic movement. If we had moved to that particular area, we would have been trapped in a snare and would have faced many problems. How good to follow the leading of the Master, instead of following the directions of men!

A very upsetting matter was the fact that we were asked to write down during two months all our expenses and to send it in to the Mission Society of the assemblies in Holland. This was required in order to fix a monthly salary, as it was already the practice to transfer each month the same amount of financial support. Names of the donors were not made known, based upon the words: "Let not thy left hand know what thy right hand doeth" (Matt.6:3). For the missionary, all donors were to be kept anonymous. The Mission was there to acknowledge the gifts and to distribute it according to the need. The missionary had to remember that "No man that warreth entangleth himself with the affairs of this life" (2 Tim.2:3). Also we had to keep in mind that the brethren of the Mission were the men appointed over this business, according to Acts 6:3, and that the believers have to lay their gifts at the feet of these men like it was done in Acts 4:37. Though the motive may have been sincere, the whole set up of this system is contrary to the Word of God. It creates a supervision by a committee of brethren, and it kills the link of fellowship which should exist between believers and assemblies on one side and the Lord's servants on the other side, and this is clearly the Scriptural principle. It is according to the Spirit's leading to provide the need of His servants. The servant of the Lord will be acquainted with the spiritual behaviour, as is set before him by the apostle Paul, the great missionary: "Let your moderation be made known TO ALL MEN ... but let your requests be made known UNTO GOD" (Phil.4:5-6).

God's School

Because of the negative experience to this point, and being burdened by the intervention of organizational tendencies from the homeland, we became more and more convinced that we were on the wrong track. While engaged in the Lord's work on the mission field we experienced the reality of Scriptural principles applied first to ourselves and then to the work of the Lord. "Take heed unto thyself and unto the doctrine, continue in them: for in doing this thou shalt both save thyself, and them that hear thee" (1 Tim.4:16). As we had to learn to trust the Lord unreservedly, all the sad and discouraging experiences became for us 'God's school'. We had to ask ourselves the all important question: "Are we the servants of men or the servants of the Lord?" The answer was clear, and in order to bring the practice into harmony with our conviction we felt led to take a far-reaching decision to sever all connections with human institutions. However, since the assemblies treated the established Mission as an authoritative institution in missionary work, it meant that from that time on we were without their financial support. It was clear that certain assemblies on the continent of Europe lost their identity as autonomous assemblies. Their endeavour in the Lord's work has become the tool to minimize the power of God's Spirit even in the local assembly. But how marvellous are the ways of the Lord! By this time missionaries commended by assemblies in Canada came to live in the Netherlands. Mr. Andrew Bergsma, Mr. Lou Swaan and Mr. Cap van de Wetering moved to Holland in 1961, 1968 and 1972 respectively. They have tried to 'strengthen the things which remain' and have opened up new areas for the Gospel.

Now it was up to us to prove ourselves as His servants, being dependent only upon the Lord. Since Japan was no more the poor and primitive country that it had been in earlier years, financially things did not become easier for the missionaries. As an industrial giant Japan had developed into a rich and prosperous country. This meant however that a US Dollar was not worth 360 Yen as in earlier years, but only 130 Yen and later even less than 100 Yen. But our God does not work with 'exchange rates'. His promise is to supply all our need. I recall that one day when we had been praying for our daily need, it happened that we received a calendar in the mail. As we turned to the page for the current day we were impressed as we read the verse: "But my God shall supply all your need according to His riches in glory by Christ Jesus" (Phil.4:19). What an encouragement to receive this promise through a small calendar page!

God's Miracles
At this point much could be mentioned concerning the Lord's miraculous provision. Each servant of the Lord will have had the experience of a need met in a miraculous way. It was not easy for us as a family in the times when we had just boiled rice on the table without anything to go with it. A most simple meal, but yet, so long as we are able to thank the Lord from our heart for it, a most simple meal tastes delicious.

Due to a serious back problem I was in hospital for three

weeks. On the day I was discharged, and obliged to pay the hospital bill in cash, Gerda came in with the needed amount of money. This provision from the Lord had been received the day before in one cheque. On another occasion when our 15-year-old daughter Linda was in hospital because of a heart condition, we discovered that on the last day of her stay somebody had come in to pay the bill. Till today we do not know who, but accepted it very gratefully as from the Lord. In whatever experience, in the small or big things of life, the Lord proved Himself to be our faithful God. We truly can say that God is still working miracles! "Casting all your care upon Him, for He careth for you" (1 Peter 5:7).

At times some individual believers and a few assemblies in the U.K., USA and Canada began to send us gifts of fellowship. Having no connection with these countries at all and at that time being unknown to these believers, the occasional letters with their financial support were like 'ravens' sent from heaven. We do not know how these Christians heard about us, but we do know why. Spiritually we have been made so rich by the caring Hand of a gracious and loving God and Father. Could we ever doubt the faithfulness of our God?

CHAPTER NINE

Canada—A New Home Country

The education of missionaries' children is one of the most difficult problems to be faced on the mission field. Often in prayer meetings the missionary's name is mentioned, but may we be challenged not to forget to pray for this particular matter. For the missionaries there may be different options such as, a correspondence course, a native school, or if available a 'foreign' school—usually an American school. Whatever decision is made, it is never right to criticise a missionary for it, as he is trying to do what is best for his children. These children unknowingly sacrifice a lot because they live in a foreign country. On the other hand they also have the advantage of living in a different culture and speaking two or more languages. Since Dutch was spoken in our home, Japanese outside and in the assembly, and English in the American school in Tokyo, our children were raised in three languages. The disadvantage for our children was to be away from home in a boarding school. How difficult it was for a six-year-old to come out of a Dutch home into a completely American environment, unable to speak one word of English! However, children learn easily and naturally, and since our children got their school education in English, it was not long before it became their first language. By the time our oldest daughter Linda graduated from high school we faced another problem: What do we do with a Dutch girl, living in Japan, who graduated from an American High school? Because of further education, the normal thing to do would be to send the children back to the homeland. Since an American high school diploma is not recognized in Holland, it would be very difficult to find an entry-point into the Dutch school system, and it would have meant a loss of at least three years.

Back in 1975 we had received invitations to come over to Canada and the USA. We appreciated the kindness, but it remained an exercise of prayer for us to arrive at the Lord's will in this matter. There is a rich blessing in store for those who wait upon the Lord and never act in a hurry. Accordingly, we waited another two years, and assured of the Lord's guidance we applied for immigration to Canada. It took some effort to get all the records together, but after we handed over the documents to the Canadian Embassy in Tokyo, we received the immigration papers within three months. When our second daughter Marion graduated from high school we made preparations for our journey to North America. It was quite exciting for us to travel to countries where we had never been. Together with Mr. and Mrs. Currie and two of their children we flew into Los Angeles, where our brother had made arrangements for us to buy a station wagon cheaply. This car served its purpose well in transporting a family of seven, together with all our luggage. On our way to Canada we were able to pass through some of the assemblies along the west coast, and in Salem, Oregon, I was privileged to preach the Gospel in English for the first time. Whether in English, Dutch or Japanese, there is no better message to proclaim!

On a beautiful sunny day in the beginning of August 1977, we crossed the border and arrived in the country of our adoption, where we were welcomed by some believers and guided to the Missionary Home in Burnaby, British Columbia. Though we had come as complete strangers, we were made very welcome by the believers, and we received so much genuine care that it was not difficult to feel at home right away. It has been our privilege to be with believers in assemblies where the presence of the Lord is felt and deeply appreciated. That is not to say that we found perfect assemblies in the new countries, for each assembly will be characterized by human weakness. Yet, we were impressed to see that the believers had a great dedication to the Lord in observing the Scriptural principles regarding gathering in the Lord's Name, and there was also much zeal in preaching the Gospel in all the assemblies with which we became acquainted.

Since the assembly at Hilversum in Holland, which originally commended us to the Lord's work, had ceased to exist, we were very thankful that assemblies in Canada and the USA were willing to re-commend us to the Lord's work, and in 1979 we left again for Japan to continue where we left off. This time, however, our family had shrunk since we left Linda and Marion behind in Canada, later followed by Carla, Monica and Robert after their graduation from the American high school in Tokyo. Eventually, our children's marriages accumulated a total of five nationalities—an international family indeed!

Becoming Canadians

As we continued in our missionary work in Japan, we faced difficulty in keeping our Canadian Immigrant Status. With a 'Returning Resident Permit' we were only allowed to be out of the country for a maximum of two years at a time. We felt this to be a limitation in our work, and in order to solve this problem we decided to apply for Canadian citizenship. Although we requested the necessary documents from the Canadian Embassy in Tokyo, we knew that we did not qualify for citizenship since we had not lived in Canada for the required number of consecutive years. When returning the documents, we included a letter addressed to the Minister of Immigration at Ottawa, explaining our circumstances as missionaries, and we politely asked for an exception in granting us the privilege of obtaining Canadian citizenship. Not long after, we received a reply in which we were asked to appear in a lawyer's office in Vancouver. In the meantime we were advised to study some facts about Canada, which were contained in a booklet we received. When we sat down at the lawyer's desk, he asked us about ten questions, and we gave the right answers except for the date of 'Canada Day', which I promptly set on July 4th instead of July 1st! We learned that our application for citizenship was not a normal procedure and that the Ministry of Immigration in Ottawa had to give special approval, and so we were asked to phone the Lawyer's Office the next day at two o'clock in the afternoon. I remember the moment so well when we heard that approval had been granted. The ceremony took place about two weeks later. Since Holland does not allow dual citizenship, we lost our Dutch citizenship, but whether Dutch, Canadian or American, the citizenship which will count for eternity is our citizenship of Heaven!

"For our citizenship is in Heaven from whence also we look for the Saviour, the Lord Jesus Christ" (Phil.3:20).

CHAPTER TEN

Holland—A New Sphere of Labour

While engaged in our missionary work in Japan, we experienced an unexpected 'Macedonian Call' toward the end of 1985. Elders from some of the Dutch and Belgian assemblies had requested, "Come over and help us". Their reasoning was: "You have given more than 30 years of your life for the Lord's work in Japan, can't you give us your help for even a few years in the Lord's work in the Netherlands and Belgium? We are in need of help." Since our roots were well established in 'the Land of the Rising Sun', and as we were blessed and encouraged in the Lord's work, it was not an easy decision to make. We took it before the Lord in prayer and also used the opportunity to bring it to the attention of our commending assemblies. We were pleased to have their full understanding in our decision to move from Japan to Holland.

There were difficult moments saying 'sayonara' to the dear Japanese believers. Though we left Japan with tears in our eyes, we did not doubt the Lord's guidance to serve Him in a new sphere of responsibility. In reviewing more than thirty years of missionary work in 'the Land of the Rising Sun', we could only utter words of thanksgiving unto Him who granted us these many years to live and to work among the Japanese.

When we arrived in Holland we were welcomed by our co-workers Lou and Trudi Swaan, who were at that time the only full-time workers in the Dutch assemblies. We came to Holland with only our personal belongings. When we had decided on our place of living, the burden was upon us to furnish the house. It happened that twelve days prior to our move, my mother went to be with the Lord at the age of nearly 96. Among the relatives it was decided that we could make use of her furniture and other belongings and when the day came to move into our new home it was furnished in a matter of a few hours. My mother possessed some nice things and we are thankful to enjoy them in remembrance of her.

As missionaries in Holland, with Mr. and Mrs. Lou Swaan

Workers together in tent meetings
God is calling you! God is looking for you!

The Great Need

Being back in Holland I could not help but think of the early years of my life, when Mr. Peter Wilson was preaching the Gospel in many areas of Holland and Belgium, this had resulted in much fruit. Many people were saved, amongst them my own parents. What a zealous endeavour in the Gospel through a preacher from Scotland! I always remain thankful to the Lord for sending His servant to Holland. Now I am here with the same task: to preach the Gospel of the Lord Jesus Christ. Though the message is the same, conditions have changed drastically. Life in the earlier days was very simple and there were many poor people. Spiritually, however, things looked bright. Nowadays Holland is a prosperous and materialistic country, but spiritually very poor. The Bible is no longer recognized as the Word of God. Due to a tolerant attitude people do not discriminate between religions and consequently all kinds of Eastern religions and occult powers are on the increase. Furthermore, churches in Holland have always been strongly influenced by Calvinistic teaching, and for that reason alone it is not an easy field for the Gospel. Today, even those churches are influenced by modern interpretations of the Bible which deny the basic doctrines of the faith. A well-known Church organization has discarded the first eleven chapters of Genesis as being fictitious. Morally the country is in bad shape. The laws are lenient, especially in view of the drug trade and its abuses. Soft drugs are partly legal. Amsterdam is the biggest drug centre for the whole of Europe. Even border cities are terrorized by drug users from Germany and Belgium. In the big cities there are churches which open their doors to distribute clean needles for drug addicts and even provide drugs. This apparently is their 'missionary work'.

Opportunities Granted

In the midst of much decline we remain thankful for assemblies which desire to keep up a good testimony for the Lord's Name. It is important to give recognition to the authority of God's Word, weak though the testimony may be. In this new sphere of labour, as I work together with Mr. Lou Swaan, we try to be a help not only to assemblies in Holland but also to a few Dutch-speaking assemblies in Belgium. Of late I was able to

A Missionary Report Meeting

preach the Gospel in tent meetings in Switzerland as well. The Lord will bless every effort to make Christ known to a lost world and the ministry to build up testimonies for His Name. How good to see the Lord's hand in blessing on His work in the different countries!

Shortly after our return to Holland we were burdened about Christians who were once in fellowship, but had left the assembly for one reason or another. We tried to give our attention to them by paying them a visit. We heard about an old brother living in Zeist. In my childhood days this family was living across the street from us, and I remembered that Mr. van der Akker was in the assembly where Mr. Peter Wilson was living. We visited this old man and started to talk about old times. I asked him how he got saved and it was such a good testimony to listen to. "What about baptism after you got saved?", was my next question. And again we heard in detail the event of his baptism. "And what about coming into the fellowship of the assembly?", was the next subject. We so much enjoyed hearing about his zeal and dedication to the Lord. He told us how he was taken along by Peter Wilson to preach the Gospel in different areas in Holland. What a life filled with joy in serving the Master! After hearing about the happy times of the past, I suddenly put the reality of the present before him. "Brother, what a blessing to hear about your life in past years, but what about NOW?" He knew what I meant and he looked at me, while he uttered: "Yes, what about now? I know I should be in assembly fellowship". Under much pressure from his first wife, who never was in the assembly, he had left the fellowship about 50 years previously. Since then he had not been happy. We opened the Scriptures and read verses concerning God's grace in restoration. We prayed together and we left him. What a joy to see him the next Lord's day coming out to the meeting! There he sat in the back seat with tears in his eyes. It was not long before he was received into the fellowship of the assembly. He enjoyed this fellowship for only a short time, then the Lord took him to be with Himself. What a great privilege to be taken Home while in assembly fellowship! Whichever way you look at it, it remains a great spiritual loss not to be in a local assembly! During the first year of our stay in Holland we saw several Christians restored to the assembly. What marvellous grace revealed in a work of restoration!

Publication Work

Another activity we took upon ourselves was the publication of an assembly magazine and books. This work requires a lot of our time, but we feel the blessed effect in so many ways. With a deep sense of gratitude we were able to publish four books, these are available in the Christian bookstores in Holland and Belgium. The computer is quite a handy tool in this work. When I acquired one the friendly salesman told me to exercise patience in learning how to use it. "It could happen, that you will be so frustrated, you may want to open the window and throw the computer out", so were his words of warning. At times I expected the computer to solve a certain problem, so I used the handy key for 'help', but—there was no help! There is another key, called 'esc', which is used when you want to escape a problem, but—there was no escape! Whatever I tried there was no solution to the problem. I did look at the window, but did not open it. "Practice makes perfect" is the saying and though I am not an expert yet, I am thankful for this helpful tool in the publishing work and could not do without it.

The Lord has His servants in the different countries, but the need remains so great. The continent from which the Gospel was once carried into the dark places all over the world has become a mission field itself. "Pray ye therefore the Lord of the harvest, that He would send forth labourers into His harvest" (Luke 10:2).

CHAPTER ELEVEN

Revisiting Japan

After a lapse of seven years we were able to revisit Japan. It started with a long distance telephone call from a Japanese brother who asked me whether we had any plans to visit our former mission field. I answered, "Yes, we have been thinking about it and it is our heart's desire to meet the dear Japanese Christians again. We are praying about it and wait for the Lord's guidance". With this telephone call we were warmly invited by a number of Japanese assemblies. It was a moment of deep emotion. Again we have seen prayers clearly answered by our faithful God! At that time the words of the great Apostle were firmly laid upon our heart: "Let us go again and visit our brethren in every city where we have preached the word of the Lord, and see how they do" (Acts 15:36).

In the beginning of January 1993 we left Holland for a longer stay in Japan. It was quite an experience to be back in the country where we had lived and worked more than 30 years for the Lord. Since we were married in Japan, and all our children were born and raised there, this country has a special place in our lives.

A Japanese brother had prepared a schedule of meetings to cover at least 35 assemblies, spread out over the four main islands. In discussing the proposed meetings he excused himself repeatedly for the heavy schedule with a meeting each night, house meetings during daytime and usually two meetings on Saturdays and three on Sundays. With Tokyo as my base, I started out to be at the annual Tokyo Conference. Mr. Jack Hay from Scotland was invited as special speaker and with an interpreter he gave excellent ministry. I was wondering how the fluency of my Japanese would be after a lapse of 7 years. When the meeting was finished and Gerda and I were together, she said she was amazed that my Japanese sounded as if I had never left the country. This was quite a compliment for which I was

主は永遠の神、地の果てまで創造された方

Assemblies in Japan: some small, some big as testimonies for the Lord's Name (see also pages 115 and 117)

8

thankful. As I felt that the Lord was giving much help, I started out with the schedule of arranged meetings in local assemblies.

The first journey brought me to snow-covered areas as far north as Hokkaido. The first stop was in a place on the west coast of Honshu. It was my joy to be there in 1985 for a series of Gospel meetings during the early stages of a new work. Today there is a small assembly of about 15 believers. It was a thrill to preach the Gospel, which resulted in the conversion of a 45 year old man. His daughter had been saved some time earlier and she had used every opportunity to witness to her father, who as the mayor's secretary is a man of great influence.

While in Hakodate on the northern island of Hokkaido, I remembered my previous stay in 1959. At that time there was no assembly, and a missionary from New Zealand, Mr. Stuart Caldwell, had just started a weekly Gospel meeting in that city. He had to take a four hour ferry across from the mainland. I remember sitting with him on the *tatami* (straw mats) in a rented room of a Japanese inn where we preached the Gospel to only two strangers, who had accepted the invitation to attend the meeting. Today Hakodate has a nice assembly with an outreach activity in other areas as well. I went further north and visited the assembly at Takigawa, where a Japanese evangelist is actively involved. It was the first time for me to be in this assembly and I enjoyed the fellowship very much.

From Hokkaido I travelled along the east coast back to Tokyo. On this stretch I enjoyed fellowship in assemblies where Mr. and Mrs. James McAllister worked for the Lord in years past. The assembly at Morioka was doing especially well as a bright testimony in that big city. In Yamagata the sight of snow-covered mountains was unforgettable. Although the assembly there is still small it is doing well in its testimony for the Lord. In addition to the meetings held in the city of Sendai, I particularly enjoyed the fellowship with the elders there. It is such a great encouragement to be able to give them advice in some of their current problems and to be of some help for the strengthening of the testimony! At Fukushima I was the guest of Mr. and Mrs. Charles Lawrence, missionaries from England, where I enjoyed fellowship in their nice Japanese home.

I concluded that first trip with meetings in the area where we had started a testimony for the Lord back in 1959. It was a great

joy to be again in these places for meetings and personal visits, as we had toiled in this area for quite a number of years, often under difficult circumstances. It was rewarding to see the Christians faithfully continue in their testimony for the Lord. The visit to Shimodate brought back sweet memories of the past, where Mrs. Ichimura was saved in 1960 as the first fruits of the work there. At the time of our visit she was 87 years old. The balm of her lovely hospitality over many years in the past has caused me to regard her as 'my mother', in the same manner as the apostle Paul saw Rufus' mother: "Greet Rufus . . . and his mother and mine" (Rom.16:13). Since we moved to Holland she has kept up a correspondence with us, and has repeatedly expressed her thankfulness for our efforts in bringing the Gospel to her house. I remember the day when she got saved and how many others followed her example through her testimony. In her life the words, "Believe on the Lord Jesus Christ, and thou shalt be saved, and thy house" (Acts 16:31), were fulfilled. Those were times of special blessing. What a reunion it was to be with these dear Christians!

On the second journey I travelled along the west coast of Honshu. In one area there are seven assemblies, established by the efforts of Japanese brethren. I was very impressed by the activity of these assemblies especially in their outreach in the different areas. There was great joy when a girl of 18 professed to be saved after a Gospel meeting. As I had opportunity to minister God's Word, and to have personal talks in the homes of Christians, it filled my heart with great satisfaction to be used as a help in the Lord's work.

The third trip took me from Tokyo to Osaka and all the way down to Kyushu, the southern main island. Again on this occasion there was the joy of witnessing the Lord's work in saving a soul. A woman of about 40 accepted the Lord Jesus as her Saviour. This happened at Hamamatsu where Mr. and Mrs. Montgomery Browne from the U.S.A. started the work in 1953, together with Mr. and Mrs. Thomas Hay. There is a thriving assembly work and I was happy to be there for Gospel and ministry meetings. Also my visit to Koo, a small town near Nagoya, was an unforgettable time of fellowship. This assembly was established in 1951, mainly through the outstanding testimony of a Japanese doctor. Dr. Ogawa got saved in Tokyo,

but opened his doctor's practice at Koo. His patients did not only get to know what was wrong physically, but also spiritually. Many experienced their salvation and in this small community the assembly has a good reputation. Mr. and Mrs. Ray Lower, who lived in Nagoya, have given much of their time and effort to give help in the Lord's work at Koo.

My stay in Japan's second biggest city Osaka started with a Gospel meeting in a rented hall in a shopping mall. I was amazed to see the hall completely filled, including a good number of strangers. While I was the guest in three assemblies, I took up subjects concerning the local assembly and practical Christian . living. The discussions which followed these meetings were lively and a proof that the ministry was a help to the believers in their zeal for the Lord. On that occasion Mrs. Doris Budd was at one of the meetings, and later in a brother's home we had a good time of fellowship. Mr. Howard Budd went to be with the Lord in 1980, and his wife in the beginning of 1994 while visiting Canada. For many years they had given themselves completely to the Lord's work in Osaka, where they found a blessed ministry in radio work.

In the southern island of Kyushu I had meetings in six assemblies. The late Mr. Harry J. Steele, who went to be with the Lord in 1985, had worked in this area for many years together with his wife Ellen. The assembly at Kita-Kyushu, formerly called Kokura, was started in 1947 through the efforts of Dr. Ishihama. This dentist later practised his dentistry in Kobe with the purpose to be of a help in the assembly there.

At a conference with three sessions of meetings, I was quite surprised to be the only speaker. Afterwards a young man came up to me and said, "Mr. Bouwman, you will not recognize me, but you are my spiritual father". I asked his name and where he was from and learned that he was one of those who got saved during my last special effort in the Gospel, held in the assembly at Kita-Kyushu, before moving to Holland. I was invited into the home of this brother for a meal. He was 30 years old then, married to a dear sister, and they had two little girls. I was impressed by his spiritual growth during the seven years; he has a great zeal to study the Bible and has a sound spiritual knowledge of Scripture. I would not be surprised if this promising young man would be called to full-time service for

Young brethren eager to study the Bible

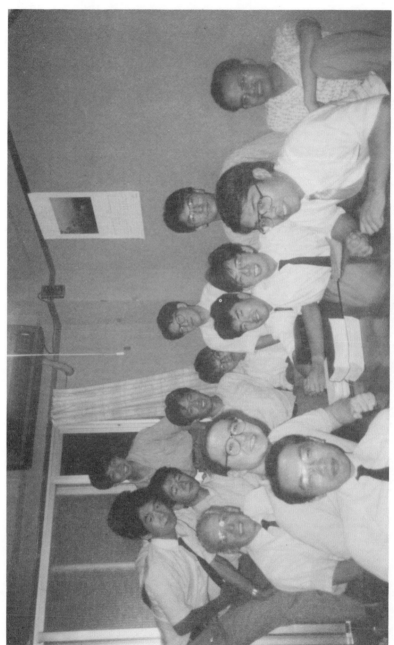

Young brethren eager to study the Bible

Sitting on the 'tatami' (straw mats) with Mrs. Ichimura, a 'mother in Israel' and her daughter-in-law

the Lord. We do pray for young brethren like him with anticipation.

The last stop on this trip was the city of Fukuoka where Mr. Johannes Rusckow from Germany started the work in 1957. He was the missionary with whom I travelled to Japan. In the early stages Johannes concentrated his efforts mainly on students and not without result. A great number of these promising young men got saved and in due time an assembly was established. With these men, now pillars in the assembly, we remembered those early days of blessing. But even now, the Lord's work is continuing quite well, and I remain thankful for the opportunity to minister the Word of God in this happy assembly.

In the Tokyo area where we know most of the Christians, six assemblies invited me for meetings. It was a thrill to see young brethren taking part in the assemblies whom we knew from childhood, and it is a credit to the parents who did the work to 'train up a child in the way he should go' (Prov.22:6). The assembly at Fuchu had grown considerably since we were last there. Here Mr. and Mrs. James Currie work for the Lord and since Jim bears the responsibility for the work of the Evangelical Publishing Depot, we found it profitable to share our mutual interest in this aspect of the work. I also met Miss Kathleen Riddles (N. Ireland), Miss Gloria Speechley (Australia) and Miss Hilda Wielenga (U.S.A.), who have shown their consistency and faithfulness in the Lord's work. Miss Speechley has been responsible for the EPD-bookshop and for editing work. This time I was not able to be in the assembly at Kyoto. For many years Miss Esther Curtin and Miss Bessie Trotter, both from England, have faithfully worked there as 'servants of the church' (Rom.16:1).

It was with a sense of deep satisfaction that I finished the scheduled meetings. In the past when we lived in Japan we were 'one of them', but in this most recent visit we became their guests, and as such, oriental hospitality dictates the royal treatment. They went out of their way to make us feel special, and their display of sacrificial hospitality followed us no matter where we went.

We were warmly thanked for spending more than 30 years of our life for the Lord's work in Japan. I was also asked to pass on the Japanese believers' sincere appreciation to those who by their prayers and support have made it possible for us to live and work in Japan to bring the Gospel to them as a manifestation of abundant grace.

CHAPTER TWELVE

Memories of a Precious Daughter

In the same year that we moved from Japan to Holland, our daughter Marion and her husband Alan moved from Canada to Japan. They believed in the Lord's call, and with a dedicated heart they not only sacrificed all their possessions, but also themselves. While Alan was zealously studying the Japanese language, it was discovered that Marion had terminal cancer. We remember receiving this shocking news, which became the precursor of so many changes. We desired to be with Marion as much as possible to give both her and her family the needed help, and soon we found ourselves together in the Missionary Home at Burnaby in Canada. During Marion's sickness, not only my wife, but also our daughters have been sacrificial in their help. We felt that being with Marion in those last days was not a burden, but on the contrary a great blessing. In her quiet spirit and loving heart there was always a sense of peace and rest. People who came to see her were encouraged and blessed and so were we, as she was completely surrendered to the will of the Lord and never voiced a complaint. Though we only had her for 29 years with us here on earth, we remain thankful for her life lived for the Lord.

Marion was going to die. She was going to leave behind not only her husband, but also her two little ones, Michelle (5) and Christopher (3). When Gerda carefully asked how she saw the future of her children, Marion answered, "Mum, I have committed them into the hand of my Lord and Saviour. The Lord Jesus will care for them much better than I ever could". The words of Marion were not empty phrases. They were the expression of her faith. She spoke about Heaven as a reality and was longing to be with the Lord Jesus.

On the evening of November 15, 1988 we were together in her room as a family. Marion had difficulty breathing and since it was easier for her in an upright position, she sat on the side of

Our daughter Marion Dora
Born at Tokyo: June 16th 1959
Died at Burnaby B.C.: November 15th 1988

her bed between Alan and myself. Her Mum was sitting in front of her and held her hands. In this manner Marion quietly and peacefully passed into the presence of the Lord. We did not even notice it. Then her Mum said: "Marion is with the Lord!" We had accompanied her to Heaven's Gate. She was privileged to enter; we had to stay behind. This was the moment of separation. There were tears, but soon we were able to give thanks unto the Lord for His gracious guidance in bringing one of His blood-bought children safely Home. "Death is swallowed up in victory. O death, where is thy sting? O grave, where is thy victory? Thanks be unto God, who giveth us the victory through our Lord Jesus Christ" (1 Cor.15:54-57). We put her body to rest on November 19th at 'Ocean View' Cemetery in Burnaby, B.C.

Some time before her death Marion wrote down her simple testimony in a notebook, which we found after she went to be with the Lord. It has been used in tracts all over Canada and the USA. It is translated into Dutch and Japanese also and has been used for the blessing of many.

Marion's Testimony

"I was born in 1959 in Tokyo, Japan. My parents have been missionaries to Japan for over 30 years and all five of their children were born there. My childhood was a happy one. When I was six I went to an English-speaking Christian school. We lived hours away from the 'Christian Academy in Japan' (CAJ), where my older sister and I boarded during the week. The next few years were lonely years. I remember being home-sick at night. If my sister would hear me cry she would crawl into bed with me and we would hug each other.

"One Spring day when I was almost eleven, something happened that changed my life. I was walking from the school to the dorm when I noticed a large cumulus cloud in the sky. The cloud looked like a large hand reaching down from Heaven. I thought, 'What if that were God's hand? What would He do with me if He reached down and picked me up? Would He put me in Heaven or put me in Hell?'

"Even though I was an obedient, fairly well-behaved child, I knew that I had no right to go to Heaven because I had not trusted Christ as my Saviour. I knew that Jesus died on the cross for people, including the Japanese, but I had never accepted it for myself. With simple faith I believed there and then that Jesus died on the cross for my sins. I walked on to the dorm, realizing nothing of the deep meaning and change that had taken place in my life. To me it was so simple. Thank God for a wonderful salvation that a child of ten or a grandmother of ninety can receive.

'He that believeth on the Son hath everlasting life; and he that believeth not the Son shall not see life, but the wrath of God abideth on him' (John 3:36).

"A few days later, I attended a Christian girl scouts' meeting at school. Somebody spoke about the ninety-nine sheep and the one that was lost. The shepherd looked for and found the lost lamb. Little plastic sheep had been hidden all over the room and we were supposed to see how many we could find. I promptly found a sheep behind the curtain of the window and sat down again. 'Marion, look for more', a lady said. 'No, THIS LAMB is the one Jesus found and that's enough', I replied. I remember feeling happy that I was saved, because Jesus found me!

'But as many as received Him, to them gave He power to become the sons of God, even to them that believe on His name' (John 1:12).

"When I was in grade six, a girl from the dorm, Kathy, died. While at her funeral I specifically prayed that the Lord would use me for His glory in my life, and even in my death.

"To sum up the next 16 years of my life briefly, I went to Canada in 1977 and continued my studies at the university. After graduating, I married my husband, Alan. In 1983 our daughter Michelle was born and in 1985 our son, Christopher. My husband and I felt that God was directing us to go to Japan as missionaries, so we left Canada in June 1986. In Japan Michelle attended a Japanese kindergarten. It was through her kindergarten that I came into contact with many mothers. Often the mothers dropped by our house for a cup of coffee. At times we had 20 Japanese people come to our home a week. Things were going well. Alan, my husband, was just 'taking off' in the language.

"On December 5th, Michelle had her kindergarten Christmas program. A Christian doctor told his testimony and of his work telling Japanese children suffering from cancer about the Lord Jesus. For some reason his talk moved me deeply and I thought,

'Maybe that's a work I can do—talk to children who have cancer or other diseases in our local hospitals.'

"Three days later I went to a doctor, for what I thought would be a routine check-up. I had been feeling quite fatigued for a while. The doctor discovered a large tumor in the colon and he ordered further tests. The next day Alan and I went to downtown Tokyo to see a cancer specialist, who was trained in the States. There they did a sono-gram of the liver and found three large tumors. 'What does this mean?', my husband asked the doctor. 'She has between three months and maybe two years to live. I advise you to go back to Canada', was the answer. Needless to say, we were totally shocked. We made the two-hour train ride back home in total silence. I knew that if I said something I would break down. Once back home we picked up our children from the neighbours and put them to bed. Then we cried, agonized, and prayed.

"The next day was Sunday and we went to the assembly to say goodbye. Monday and Tuesday were hectic days. With the help of friends we packed most of our clothes and they packed the rest to put everything in storage. The telephone rang constantly as the news spread and people were dropping in to say goodbye. Thank God for friends! We could not have done everything without them. On Wednesday we flew back to Canada.

"Since coming to Canada, I have had surgery and several chemo treatments. Physically, the cancer is getting worse. Spiritually, I am happy. I have joy and peace. I have experienced the love of Christians. Christians from all over have prayed for me and have really cared. My family has been so supportive. Even my little children minister to me in their own way. Little three-year-old Christopher saying: 'I love you, Mummy' many times a day while giving me a hug. Five-year-old Michelle tells me that while alone at night, she prays 'lots and lots and lots', that I would get better. 'What if I don't?', I asked her. 'But Mum, then you'll be better in Heaven.'

"I have lived a happy life. I pray that God would use my death to speak to people. God is love. He never forsakes. He is kind. Live for Him!

'For I am persuaded that neither death, nor life, nor angels, nor principalities, nor powers, nor things present, nor things to come, nor height, nor depth, nor any other creation, shall be able to separate us from the love of God, which is in Christ Jesus, our Lord' (Romans 8:38-39)."

October 1988

Alan's Words of Appreciation

Words of appreciation by Alan Essex, written after the loss of his wife Marion:

We are all very thankful to the Lord that Marion's passing into His presence was quiet and peaceful. She was spared from a lot of the suffering many cancer patients must endure. Peacefully, while sitting in the arms of her family, the Lord took her to be with Himself.

We are thankful that she was able to remain at home rather than having to be put into hospital. This gave the family many opportunities to spend quality time with her over the last number of months. We praise our wonderful Saviour that she is free from suffering and that she is now "Absent from the body and present with the Lord". It has given all of us a greater realization that very soon "The Lord Himself will descend from Heaven with a shout". What a great and glorious day it will be when we will all be together around the Throne to behold the One who gave His life for our sins and who redeemed us with His own precious blood!

Our sincere prayer is that Marion's Homecall will continue to bring honour and glory to His blessed Name and that her testimony would be used of the Lord to encourage the saints and further the purposes of the Lord in these last days. Marion was a great example of courage and patience during her time of sickness. Hers is the victory, and she will always be lovingly remembered by her quiet spirit of faith and trust in the sovereignty of the Lord's will in her life. The Scripture teaches that, "The voice of the Lord is above many waters" and despite the depth of her suffering she proved that the Lord could give the needed grace to suffer patiently and calmly.

CHAPTER THIRTEEN

Conclusion

Scriptural Principles

The Bible is a book of authority. It is the living Word of the living God. Christians all over the world from whatever cultural influence need to be guided by the authority of God's Word. In all circumstances of life the Bible is the Christian's Guide Book.

The authority of Scripture should also be recognized in view of the Lord's work. The principles of God's Word are applied in local assemblies, but sometimes when it comes to the Lord's work abroad a more lenient attitude is adopted and Scriptural principles seem to be irrelevant. Following the example of the apostle Paul, we indeed rejoice wherever Christ is preached (Phil.1:18). However, this does not mean that we should be actively involved with all kinds of Missions simply because Christ is preached. When the disciples approached the Lord Jesus with a question concerning a work done by an 'outsider', the Lord rebuked them with the words, "Forbid him not; for he that is not against us is for us" (Luke 9:50). The Lord did not say however: "Leave me and join this man in what he is doing". The disciples realized a further truth—that of valuing the tremendous privilege of following the Lord and enjoying His presence. "If any man serve me, let him follow me; and where I am, there shall also my servant be" (John 12:26).

The Lord's Call

What does Scripture teach us concerning missionary work? The beginning of missionary endeavour is recorded in Acts 13:1-4. We discover there a marvellous work done by the Holy Spirit, who is in the picture from beginning to end. The persons whom the Lord wanted to use were believers, equipped with spiritual gifts and completely dedicated to the Lord. Being among the five prophets and teachers ministering in the church at Antioch, Saul and Barnabas were already actively involved in the Lord's work. However, from that point on there was a further call to go to distant places to proclaim the blessed Gospel of the Lord Jesus Christ. This resulted not only in the salvation of precious souls, but also in the establishment of assemblies. It is the fulfilment of God's great command to preach, to baptize and to teach (Matt.28:19-20).

Considering God's plan of missionary endeavour described in the first verses of Acts 13 we discover some important facts. We see that the Holy Spirit did His work in:
1. setting out the plan (Acts 13:2)
2. selecting the persons (Acts 13:2)
3. sending out His servants (Acts 13:4)

Responsibility of the Assembly

Acts 13 indicates that missionary work involves not only individual persons called to serve the Lord, but also the entire local assembly. It was a great responsibility on the part of the assembly at Antioch to separate two of their valuable brethren for the work of the Lord (Acts 13:2). Probably the voice of the Spirit was heard by way of one of the prophets. Like the gift of 'apostle' the gift of 'prophet' belongs to the transitional period, and therefore the two gifts are usually mentioned together. In this connection the verse in Eph.2:20 shows clearly that these gifts were used to lay the foundation: "And are built upon the foundation of the apostles and prophets". At the time of the church in Antioch the New Testament had not yet been written. In those days the gift of 'prophet' was needed to pass on the oracles of God, needed for action in that particular situation.

The church at Antioch acted upon hearing the voice of the Spirit in a fourfold way:
1. they fasted—they turned away from worldly things;
2. they prayed—they turned to God;
3. they laid hands on them—they identified themselves with the servants, who were called by the Lord;
4. they sent them away—they let them go.

It is valuable to notice that the leading of the Holy Spirit in the church at Antioch was never meant to ordain, but to commend their brethren to the grace of God for the work they were called to do. In the whole of the Scriptures there is no foundation for ordaining someone to fulfil an office, as is practised in

denominational churches. It is always a work of God Himself in
calling the vessels He needs for a particular work. This is also
the case with regard to the work of elders in a local assembly.
"Take heed therefore unto yourselves, and to all the flock (the
local assembly), over which the Holy Ghost hath made you
overseers, to feed the church of God (the local assembly)" (Acts
20:28).

Commendation

The subject of commendation for the Lord's work is a solemn
subject but, sadly, treated lightly in the days in which we live.
Commendation cannot be given by an organization, like a
Mission board or by a kind of central oversight of brethren
standing above a number of assemblies. Only a local assembly
has the authority to commend a servant of the Lord. In giving
commendation the assembly recognizes what God is doing. It
means that the assembly is putting its full trust and confidence
in the Lord's servants in all their movements, being assured that
the Lord has called them. An assembly can have a 'farewell-
meeting' for them, but the 'sending out' is done by the Lord
Himself. The assembly lets them go, realizing that the Lord's
servants are called and sent forth by the Holy Spirit (Acts
13:2,4).

A Work of God

Where God is at work there is a great work done! His servants
were:
—called by the Holy Spirit (Acts 13:2),
—sent forth by the Holy Spirit (Acts 13:4),
—guided by the Holy Spirit (Acts 16:7; 18:5; etc.),
—cared for by the Lord Himself (Phil.4:18-19).

These are the principles clearly set forth in His Word. If the
Lord calls and sends out His servants, He will take care of them.
His servants should not be indebted to unbelievers—"For His
Name's sake they went forth, taking nothing of the Gentiles" (3
John v.7). The privilege of giving for the Lord's work is granted
only to believers and to assemblies. As co-workers with God it is
a great blessing to have a part in His work here on earth. This
participation is called 'fellowship', and in this fellowship the
donors give 'as unto the Lord', and the Lord's servants receive

Serving the best of Masters,
with great gratitude for the prayers of the Lord's people

'as from the Lord'. The apostle Paul gave credit to the assembly
at Philippi "for their fellowship in the Gospel from the first day
till now" (Phil.1:5). This fellowship was shown in their prayers
of intercession and in material help rendered. What a
tremendous evaluation the Spirit of God expresses of the saints
in Philippi: "Not because I desire a gift, but I desire fruit that may
abound to your account. The things which were sent from you,
are an odour of a sweet smell, a sacrifice acceptable, wellpleasing
to God" (Phil.4:17-18). Paul did not so much 'thank' the
Philippian believers, but he described what the gift meant to
them as donors. All that we do for the Lord is recorded in
Heaven. What condescension, that the Lord deigns to use
human vessels for the salvation of the lost! "How then shall they
call on Him in whom they have not believed? And how shall they
believe in Him of whom they have not heard? And how shalll
they hear without a preacher? And how shall they preach,
EXCEPT THEY BE SENT? As it is written: How beautiful are
the feet of them that preach the Gospel of peace, and bring glad
tidings of good things!" (Romans 10:14-15).

To review the endeavour of missionary work, according to
the principles of Scriptures, there are two essential things:
1. a call from the Lord,
2. commendation from an assembly.

The exercised believer should be careful not to go out:
—without a call from the Lord;
—without commendation of an assembly;
—without having the right motivation;
—relying upon personal impressions or emotional feelings.

Although we are not living in apostolic times, it must still be a
work of the Holy Spirit from beginning to end. What is needed
for the continuation of His work here on earth is not so much
the introduction of new methods, but the need for young
Christians called by the Lord to go out and preach the Gospel.

Heaven's Reward

What a perfect and most wonderful mosaic will be manifested
in Heaven in a future day! The life of each redeemed soul,
whatever its length while here on earth, will perfectly fit into
this pattern. The review before the Judgment Seat of Christ will
not be for success, but for faithfulness. In using the word

'HOW' the apostle Paul puts the emphasis on the quality of our life and work:

"... HOW ye ought to walk and to please God" (1 Thess.4:1);

"... But let every man take heed HOW he buildeth on it" (1 Cor.3:10).

Looking back over forty years of service for the Lord and in all the guidance received—in times of joy and sorrow, prosperity and poverty, strength and weakness, victory and defeat—the Lord has proved His unchangeable faithfulness, so that we marvel at His abundant grace.

> How I praise Thee, precious Saviour!
>   That Thy love laid hold on me;
> Thou hast saved and cleansed and filled me,
>   That I might Thy channel be.
>
> Just a channel, full of blessing,
>   To the thirsty hearts around;
> To tell out Thy full salvation,
>   All Thy loving message sound.
>
> Emptied that Thou shouldest fill me,
>   A clean vessel in Thine hand;
> With no power but as Thou givest
>   Graciously with each command.
>
> Witnessing Thy power to save me,
>   Setting free from self and sin,
> Thou hast bought me to possess me,
>   In Thy fulness, Lord, come in.
>
> Channels only, blessed Master,
>   But with all Thy wondrous power
> Flowing through us, Thou canst use us
>   Every day and every hour.
>   (Believers Hymn Book—no.393)